Maggie Brown
21/11/06

THE KILBRANDON REPORT

Children in Society Series

Edited by Stewart Asquith

Other titles:
Supporting Families
Families and the Future

THE KILBRANDON REPORT

CHILDREN AND YOUNG PERSONS SCOTLAND

Foreword by

Lord Fraser of Carmyllie

Introduction by

Professor Fred H. Stone

Series Editor: Stewart Asquith

HMSO: EDINBURGH

Applications for reproduction should be made to HMSO
British Library Cataloguing in Publication Data
A catalogue record for this book is available from the British Library

ISBN 0 11 495737 1

CONTENTS

PREFACE

The Kilbrandon Report was, and still remains, one of the most influential policy statements on how a society should deal with "children in trouble". Though it is now over thirty years since it was first published, current debate about child care practices and polices in Scotland with a new Children (Scotland) Bill imminent, still resonates with principles and philosophies derived from the Kilbrandon Report itself. What is also remarkable is that the institutional framework for supporting children and families established on the basis of the key recommendations of the report has been largely unchanged since it was introduced in 1971.

Reprinting the report is then both important because of the direction it gave to child care all those years ago, and timely, in the light of changes introduced in law through the Children (Scotland) Act 1995. However, it took a chance suggestion by Sally Kuenssberg, herself actively involved in the provision of training for the Children's Hearings, to point out the difficulty of obtaining a copy of one of the most important documents in the history of Scottish child welfare. The whole process of reprinting the report would not have begun had it not been for her suggestion, and she is due many thanks.

The link with the original report is, of course, strengthened through the introduction for the reprint written by Emeritus Prof. Fred Stone, who was himself one of the members of the Kilbrandon Committee and who has contributed so much to the development of the Scottish Children's Hearings system through his writing and involvement in training.

In reprinting the report a decision was made to reproduce the text in a format as near the original as possible, to maintain a degree of historical authenticity. Appearing as it does, however, in the *Children in Society* series, an index has been added to the reprint to further assist those who may be less familiar with the contents. I feel particularly proud that the report has been reprinted in the *Children in Society* series and I am confident that its availability will be greatly appreciated by the wider readership it should thereby reach.

Professor Stewart Asquith
General Series Editor

FOREWORD

The Kilbrandon Report is a remarkable document. It was remarkable in its time and it still reads as a clear, fresh and enlightened document more than thirty years later. Few Government reports are reprinted not once, but twice, after their original publication. This is a tribute to the historical importance, the readability and the continued relevance of Lord Kilbrandon's report.

In May 1961, John Maclay, then Secretary of State for Scotland and later Lord Muirshiel, appointed a committee "to consider the provisions of the law of Scotland relating to the treatment of juvenile delinquents and juveniles in need of care or protection or beyond parental control". It was chaired by a distinguished lawyer and judge, James Shaw, Lord Kilbrandon. It contained in its membership two sheriffs, a professor of law, a solicitor, a headmaster, a chief constable, justices of the peace and a child psychiatrist.

The approach and style of the report reflect the composition of the committee. It is crisp and matter of fact. However, despite the apparently traditional membership, its recommendations were radical, humane and far-reaching. They have profoundly affected the way in which we approach children's problems in Scotland. In its conclusions, the committee set out the principles which underlie the establishment of one of our most remarkable institutions, the Children's Hearings. The report and the underlying principles are still the touchstone against which the work of the hearings is tested.

The key principles underlying the committee's proposals were: separation between the establishment of issues of disputed fact and decisions on the treatment of the child; the use of a lay panel to reach decisions on treatment; the recognition of the needs of the child as being the first and primary consideration; the vital role of the family in tackling children's problems; and the adoption of a preventive and educational approach to these problems.

It was these key principles which led Lord Hope, the present Lord President of the Court of Session, to refer in a recent judgement to "the genius of this reform [the Kilbrandon Report] which has earned it so much praise".

While the reprint of Lord Kilbrandon's report, and the continued reference to it by those who work in and discuss the Children's Hearings system, demonstrate its continuing relevance, it is necessary to prevent the system standing still or becoming fossilised.

The continuing support of the Children's Hearings through healthy recruitment, general public acceptability and the development of training and practice, demonstrate the vigour of the system. It has certainly not stood still and it has had to deal with increasingly difficult challenges.

In the early days the system was largely concerned with juveniles offending and in trouble. Latterly, increasing numbers of children who require care and protection have been referred to the hearings.

This change has been associated with a growing awareness that the interests of parents and children are not always the same. Greater emphasis is now given to listening to children and young people and taking account of their views. We have encouraged, through Scottish Office grants, the development of organisations which reflect the views of children, such as Childline and "Who Cares". I was particularly pleased that young people from the "Who Cares" organisation gave evidence directly to a committee of the House of Commons considering the Children (Scotland) Bill under our new procedures for Scottish legislation. Other developments have included the publication by us of children's views on child care law and the Children's Hearings. We look forward to the findings of the major research study commissioned by the Scottish Office and conducted by Edinburgh and Stirling Universities, evaluating the Children's Hearings system. It will include the views of children and families on their involvement in the Children's Hearings system.

These developments highlight the importance of reviewing the work of panels and the legal arrangements under which they operate. The Child Care Law Review looked closely at the work of the Children's Hearings and the report by Alan Finlayson on the work of the Reporter has contributed to the development of that service. The White Paper *Scotland's Children* published in 1993 sets out proposals for child care policy and law. The Children (Scotland) Bill which followed the White Paper will be the first major piece of legislation dealing with children since the Social Work (Scotland) Act 1968 which enacted the Kilbrandon reforms. The Bill contains many new provisions but also remains true to the original Kilbrandon principles.

The re-issue of the Kilbrandon Report comes at a time of major activity in the field of child care law. It is therefore fitting that the report from which so much of our present arrangements spring should be readily available alongside the new legislation.

Fraser of Carmyllie

INTRODUCTION

Professor Fred H. Stone

I t is almost exactly a quarter of a century since the Scottish Children's Hearings were first convened, of itself a good reason for the reprinting of the Kilbrandon Report which gave rise to a new direction in dealing with our children and young people. To have survived till now with only minor changes is an occasion for modest celebration, confounding the critics who, at the outset, predicted its early demise! It is, moreover, particularly relevant to have the report available from HMSO at a time when child care legislation is under review, with possible implications for the practice of the Children's Hearings system.

The working party, under the chairmanship of Lord Kilbrandon, first met in 1961; its unanimous recommendations were published in 1964, and were embodied in Scottish legislation by 1968, though, as we shall see, with some important amendments. Nevertheless, this was a remarkable achievement, the implications of which could hardly have been anticipated from the official remit. For those of us who had the privilege of serving on the Kilbrandon Committee, these rapid developments were a matter of some surprise and satisfaction. One must, however, admit to some misgiving about the status which the report has achieved in the intervening years, amounting almost to a sacred text in the regard of some supporters of the Children's Hearings system. In one particular respect, however, acknowledgement is long overdue, namely, the elegance and clarity of the actual writing – not all that frequent in official publications!

The Kilbrandon principles

A useful starting point is to identify the principles on which the recommendations of the report were based, and how the committee understood their task. In the words of Lord Kilbrandon himself (1966), the primary concern was with "children in trouble". He was quite explicit in identifying the major categories as a) those with delinquent behaviour, b) those in need of care or protection, c) those beyond parental control, and d) those who persistently truant.

Clearly, this was a much broader consideration than simply "delinquency", but all these children had shared a common experience, a failure in the normal experiences of upbringing. The associated principle which underpinned all proposed measures of assessment and treatment was that the paramount consideration was the welfare of the child. And for such measures to be effective, the child had to be viewed in the context of the family.

The children, young people and families under consideration, to whichever category they might be assigned, would ordinarily have sought help from available agencies, health visitor, school psychologist, general practitioner, local police, or voluntary agency such as the Royal Scottish Society for the Prevention of Cruelty to Children.* The committee's concern was about situations where ordinary, voluntary measures had for whatever reason failed, or were likely to fail. In the past, such problems tended to find their way to disciplinary tribunals of the education authority, to a police warning, to a Juvenile Court, few in number in Scotland, or, most frequently, to the local Sheriff Court. Of the many informed witnesses who gave evidence to the Kilbrandon Committee, on one point there was complete agreement, that the current arrangements for dealing with children were unsatisfactory.

The radical proposal, which was in due course put into practice, was to remove children under sixteen years of age from adult criminal procedures, with the exception of extremely severe offences, and to bring all cases in need of "compulsory measures of care" before a lay panel of three members, the Children's Hearing. This, it was judged, would provide the necessary conditions for satisfactory assessment and appropriate disposal, namely: an informal, relaxed setting, with reasonably skilled interviewers provided with reliable background information, with adequate time to promote effective communication between all concerned, and especially, an atmosphere conducive to the child's participation.

One further Kilbrandon principle must be mentioned, how the child and family were to be helped. As the common factor underlying most of the cases was a "failure of upbringing", of "social education", the remedy would need to be a form of re-education of the child, and where appropriate of the parents. It must be admitted that the report was not very explicit about how this re-educative supervision was to be achieved, though fines or other forms of sanction were considered to be incompatible with methods of help depending greatly on co-operation. What was clear, however, was the intention that the "treatment authority" would cease to be "a small and specialised part of the criminal jurisdiction, but instead ... a small but important part of the system of social service" (Kilbrandon, 1966). As is customary, legislation was preceded by a discussion document or White Paper, *Social Work and the Community* (cmnd., 1966) which proposed a reorganisation of social work in the form of autonomous departments,

* Now called Children 1st

serving all age groups and many other community needs, including the provision of reports and supervision duties for the Children's Hearings. And this was the arrangement which emerged in legislation (Social Work Scotland Act, 1968) rather than that proposed in the report, namely a new department within the education authorities.

Scotland was not the first country to create a body separate from the courts with the responsibility of making decisions in the best interests of the child. In Scandinavia, the Children's Welfare Boards had for some time pursued a welfare approach, and their use of lay board members with apparent success was known to the Kilbrandon Committee. Here again, however, the final plan had a somewhat different emphasis from that originally envisaged. From the rather brief account of the qualities expected of those to serve on the panels, the profile resembled those who had previously served on the juvenile courts, individuals with a commitment to child welfare with previous experience in this field. The final version, however, aimed at a panel recruited locally with a background and occupational spread representative of that locality, an aim which has only been partially achieved.

The actual procedures followed in the Hearings, however, have continued along the lines described in the report. Which children, or more accurately which families, enter the system is entirely the responsibility of the central official, the Reporter to the Children's Panel, who makes the prediction that "compulsory measures of care" will be required, a term which was intended to include protection, control, and guidance, as well as treatment.

In considering appropriate procedures and measures for children, the report faced the difficult task of taking into account the developmental factor, how far a particular child had progressed in understanding, in social awareness, in being held responsible for his or her actions. The traditional legal approach has been to identify a precise age as the "Age of Criminal Responsibility", in recent times in Scotland, eight years of age. After detailed discussion, the report recommended that this arbitrary age, differing widely from one country to another, and having no clinical reality, should be abandoned. This was one of the few proposals which was not accepted.

Twenty-five years on

Before embarking on a review of the Hearings' first quarter-century, account must be taken of the massive changes which have taken place during that time in Scottish family life, and especially what these changes have meant for the role of parents and the experiences of children. In many ways it is a sombre picture. In recent years about one in four marriages have ended in separation or divorce. It has become commonplace for couples to set up home and produce offspring without the formality of marriage ties, religious or secular. New liaisons often take place, so that children find themselves with multiple relationships, and lacking continuity of care. The single parent family, usually mother and child or children, not rarely with transient partnerships, is frequent, not only because the father has left the home, but because the mother has chosen to raise children by herself. Another feature, and a related one, has been the marked change in sexual mores for large sections of the population. Early sexual experience is common in both males and females, at least partly due to the availability of effective contraceptives. There is less secrecy and inhibition about sexual matters, and less stigma attached to illegitimacy. Yet many families rely on schools to provide sexual education for their children. The abuse of alcohol has remained a major problem in Scotland, and is frequently associated with violence by men towards women, adults towards children, and young people towards other members of the public. A significant proportion of schoolchildren are cigarette smokers; drug and solvent abuse is no longer rare, even at primary school level, with serious implications for health, behaviour, and, at times, survival. These decades, moreover, have been characterised throughout the United Kingdom by poor prospects of employment for many young people, and while child neglect, child abuse, truancy, delinquency, and family discord and disruption are not confined to lower income groups, poverty is a commonly associated factor.

Child-abuse cases are often complex and extremely emotive for professional as well as lay workers, and as a result have over the years made increasing demands on the time and personal resources of Reporters, panel members, and social workers. During the early years of the Hearings system such cases were quite rare; of late, the proportion of non-offence cases referred to the Reporters has risen from about a fifth to nearly half, many of them involving very young children. Not surprisingly, there has been some concern expressed whether this trend has been to the disadvantage of the offender group, which was the primary concern of the Kilbrandon Committee. And, in particular, about those over 16 years, few of whom have benefited from the Hearing's discretion to extend their supervision for a further two years. Perhaps consideration of the style and setting of the Hearings would benefit both the oldest and the youngest who attend.

The Children's Hearings system has not lacked its critics. It has been suggested that the appointees to the panels are not sufficiently representative of the families before them, being weighted towards middle-class, professional people. It is true that there has been difficulty in attracting applications from the less advantaged, from ethnic minorities, from young adults, and in some places, from males. But the advisory committees responsible for selection have gradually achieved a broader spread of recruitment. It has been asserted that in contrast to the courts, the

Hearings are viewed as a "soft option". By and large this has not proved to be the opinion of the police nor of the judges. What has to be acknowledged is that too many members of the public have little knowledge of the Children's Hearings system. And inevitably, cases successfully managed by Hearings and effectively supervised by social workers are seldom newsworthy, whereas the relatively few problematic outcomes have tended to receive widespread publicity. It is striking that both north and south of the Border, public enquiries have taken place almost exclusively in connection with "Care and Protection" situations.

From the outset, both child and parent may arrange to be accompanied to the Hearing by a "friend", companion, relative or solicitor, and many have chosen to do so. This, however, has not satisfied some critics, because this does not include formal legal representation, partly because legal aid is not available at this stage. Proposals to formalise legal participation have been resisted because an adversarial ethos would be at odds with the informality and maximal participation of child, family, and others. Such a change would, it is believed, recreate a form of court, which would seem to negate the central Kilbrandon principle. There is little doubt that this issue will continue to be debated. Attempts to introduce a more punitive approach in the management of young offenders and their families, as proposed in 1980 following the publication of the English White Paper *Young Offenders*, were firmly rejected in Scotland after consultation.

A new development in the mid-eighties (Children's Hearing Rules, 1985), was the introduction of "Safeguarders", primarily to meet situations where a conflict of interest was thought to exist between child and parents. Of the hundred or so appointed till now, either by the sheriff or the Hearing, the majority are solicitors, others mainly social workers. The Safeguarder is intended to be an independent mediator, representing the interests of the child. The first national seminar reviewing the role and function of the Safeguarder was held in 1993, where consideration was given to issues of selection, training, and accountability. This is an evolving activity, and is likely to be an important item of future legislation.

The imminent reorganisation of Scottish local authorities involving the creation of many autonomous bodies, gives some concern about the availability of adequate childcare resources throughout the country, in particular those required to meet the recommendations of Children's Hearings. Moreover, the internal reorganisation of the Reporter Service, which has just taken place, replacing a local by a national body, under the direction of a Principal Reporter for Scotland, makes inevitable a further readjustment for the Hearings system. It is fair to state, however, that since its inauguration, the Children's Hearings system has never stood still, and has coped remarkably well with changing demands. In 1988 the Secretary of State initiated a review of child care law in Scotland which, although suggesting many improvements, did not consider that any radical changes were required. The following year the United Nations General Assembly adopted its *Convention on the Rights of the Child*, which has been ratified by the UK but which reserves its right "to continue the present operation of Children's Hearings". However, whereas there continues to be strong support from many quarters for the preservation of the essentially non-adversarial approach of the Hearings, there may well be changes in procedures involving the removal of a child from his or her family, or the taking over of parental rights by a local authority, both of which are likely to require the sanction of a court. The call for legislative changes affecting child care has arisen also from two Scottish enquiries in Fife and Orkney, whose findings were both published in 1992 as the Kearney and Clyde Reports respectively. The former was concerned to improve mutual respect and co-operation between a social work department and its related Children's Hearings service; the latter to improve procedures by all the authorities involved when the removal of children to a "place of safety" was contemplated. Other considerations which have come to the fore of late have mainly aimed to improve the quality of the Hearings themselves by increased flexibility and discretionary powers of the chairperson. The opportunity to implement new legislation regarding these and other related child-care issues arises timeously with the Children (Scotland) Act 1995.

Does the Scottish Children's Hearings system work? One answer must surely be that for an innovative, even radical system of juvenile justice to have continued for twenty-five years with few modifications, mainly in response to changing social conditions, is reassuring. As far as the public interest is concerned, there is no evidence that the removal of most delinquent children and adolescents from the jurisdiction of the courts has resulted in an escalation of antisocial behaviour. It is worth recalling that the starting point of the deliberations of the Kilbrandon Committee was the widespread dissatisfaction with court-centred procedures involving children, as these were frequently experienced as intimidating and poorly understood. Whatever the shortcomings of some Hearings, time is made available for careful assessment of problems, with the benefit of social background and educational reports, and, when indicated, the opinion of a children's specialist, with encouragement and opportunity for participation of child and parents. Yet Hearings have considerable powers, so it is hardly surprising that those attending may be anxious. Reporters and others take pains to ensure that children and adults are given clear explanations of what is taking place, with the help of information pamphlets. A particular merit of the Hearings system is the requirement to arrange a follow-up review within twelve months, but regrettably this does not always ensure continuity of panel membership. Chairpersons have always had the power to exclude a child from all or part of a hearing. A clear view expressed by older children is the wish to be allowed at least part of the hearing without the parents' presence, a sensible provision which is likely to be introduced.

It is encouraging to note that the Social Work Services Group has initiated research into the workings of the Hearings system on two fronts: a) factors involved in decision making, and b) a longitudinal study examining outcomes for a cohort of referred children. There will be no shortage of pressing research topics in the future. For example, we need to learn more about the techniques employed in the selection of panel members, whether special aptitudes are required for different types of child and family problems; in view of the continuing loss of quite a few panel members after relatively short periods of service, whether a probationary appointment should be routine. We also require information about the range of methods and skills employed in the supervision of children and adolescents, and the resources of proven value as yet unavailable. In England and Wales, the system of juvenile justice, while sharing essentially similar aims with Scotland, has continued to deal with young offenders in juvenile courts, and, with "Care and Protection" situations, in family proceeding courts, involving solicitors and guardians *ad litem* (Children Act, 1989). An opportunity is thereby presented for a potentially valuable study of the relative merits of the two approaches.

This overview would not be complete without special mention of the lay members of the Children's Panels. Volunteers have continued to come forward, to submit themselves to quite stringent methods of selection, to participate in training sessions, and to have their performance regularly monitored. The enthusiasm and commitment of the majority has been notable, and over 10,000 have been appointed during the past twenty years.

References

British Journal of Criminology, VI, Children in Trouble, p112–122, 1966. Shaw, J., Lord Kilbrandon.

Social Work and Community Cmnd, 3065, October 1966.

The Report of the Inquiry into Child Care Policies in Fife, Kearney B. and Mapstone E. L. G. (1992) Edinburgh: HMSO.

The Report of the Inquiry into the Removal of Children from Orkney in February, 1991. Clyde J. J. (1992) Edinburgh: HMSO.

The Children Act (1989) HMSO.

SCOTTISH HOME AND HEALTH DEPARTMENT
SCOTTISH EDUCATION DEPARTMENT

Children
and Young Persons
SCOTLAND

REPORT BY THE COMMITTEE
APPOINTED BY THE SECRETARY OF STATE
FOR SCOTLAND

*Presented to Parliament by the Secretary of State for Scotland
by Command of Her Majesty
April, 1964*

EDINBURGH
HER MAJESTY'S STATIONERY OFFICE

CONTENTS

3

Part Three

Appendices

Children and Young Persons, Scotland

To the Right Honourable MICHAEL ANTONY CRISTOBAL NOBLE, M.P.,
Secretary of State for Scotland

Introduction

REMIT

1.   We were appointed by your predecessor, the Rt. Hon. John S. Maclay, C.H.,
C.M.G., M.P., on 29th May, 1961, with the following remit:

> "to consider the provisions of the law of Scotland relating to the treatment
> of juvenile delinquents and juveniles in need of care or protection or
> beyond parental control and, in particular, the constitution, powers and
> procedure of the courts dealing with such juveniles, and to report."

We now submit our report. Our remit covered a wide field, but our task has
been appreciably lightened by the separate inquiries into specific subjects,
already carried out under the auspices of your Advisory Councils on the
Treatment of Offenders and on Child Care, and extending to the custodial
treatment of young offenders, borstal training, remand homes, and the
prevention of neglect of children in their own homes. Many of the Councils'
recommendations have already been given effect in the Criminal Justice
(Scotland) Act, and the Children and Young Persons Act, 1963.

PROCEDURE

2.   At the outset we extended a general invitation by way of press notice to
submit written evidence and in addition sent invitations to a number of persons
and organisations to do so. As a result, we received a considerable number of
written statements and we later heard oral evidence on 15 days from persons
giving evidence either in a personal capacity or as representing various
organisations. A list of the witnesses is set out in Appendix E. We were also
assisted by several factual memoranda from the Scottish Home and Health
Department and the Scottish Education Department.

3.   We have met on 29 days. In addition, we have, either individually or in
groups, visited a substantial number of juvenile courts as well as a variety of
residential institutions (including several in England) to which children are
committed by the juvenile courts. We are indebted to the Norwegian Ministry of
Social Affairs, the Director of the Danish Institute, Edinburgh, and Dr. Ola
Nyquist (Assistant Professor of Criminal Policy, University of Uppsala), for
information and assistance bearing on the Scandinavian systems of child welfare
committees or boards; and to Mr. John Mack, Director of Social Study, Glasgow
University, for information derived from his research studies on police juvenile
liaison schemes. We should like to record our thanks to all those who have
helped us by the submission of views and information, orally or in writing.

4. We desire to express our sincere gratitude for the admirable work done by Mr. A. T. F. Ogilvie, our Secretary. He was a mine of accurate information, presented always with a freshness of outlook and a breadth of vision which were of the greatest possible assistance to us. We also wish to thank Mr. R. J. Edie, our Assistant Secretary, whose knowledge of various fields of work within the sphere of the Scottish Education Department was invaluable, as also was his help in recording our proceedings and especially the oral evidence.

Part One

CHAPTER I

The Basic Problem: Its Scope and the Practical Issues Arising

INTRODUCTORY

5.   Our remit refers to "juvenile delinquents and juveniles in need of care or protection or beyond parental control". Juvenile delinquents and juveniles in need of care or protection or beyond parental control, we take to mean broadly those juveniles who may in certain specified situations or circumstances be brought before a juvenile court. The law recognises four such groups—juveniles alleged to have committed crimes or offences, children in need of care or protection, children who are refractory or beyond parental control, and children who are persistent truants. In any of these situations, if the facts and circumstances alleged are proved to the satisfaction of the court, the children concerned may be the subject of court orders, involving compulsory measures which may in greater or lesser degree entail infringement of personal liberty and of parental rights. By law juvenile offenders comprise offenders aged 8 or over and under 17; a juvenile of any age under 17 may be the subject of care or protection proceedings or proceedings arising from refractory conduct as being beyond parental control. Proceedings arising from persistent truancy may be applied to any child of school age.

THE CHILDREN APPEARING BEFORE THE COURTS

Juvenile offenders

6.   The criminal law proceeds on the basis that crimes and offences carry a liability to prosecution, and, if proved before a court of law, a liability to certain penalties. An offence once detected does not, however, necessarily result in prosecution—a traditional and basic feature of the law being that (exceptional cases of private prosecution apart) in each case the decision whether or not to prosecute lies with an independent public prosecutor acting in the public interest. In each case it is his duty, and his alone, to consider not only whether there is sufficient evidence to support the prosecution, but also whether the case is of such a nature that the public interest demands prosecution. Given the tremendous range of acts recognised as offences under statute or common law, it is plain that in practice the police have always—and necessarily—exercised some measure of discretion, at a variety of levels, in the reporting of alleged offences, and that equally prosecutors for their part may, on considering reports made to them, decide not to institute proceedings, and sometimes to deal with the matter by warning. These factors are common to the consideration of proceedings in respect of offenders of all ages, but have for long been recognised as having particular application to children, and clearly any

assessment of the volume of juvenile delinquency must take account of the effect of these preliminary sifting processes.

7. The published Criminal Statistics, which record the number of juveniles proceeded against and dealt with by the courts, need to be studied with caution particularly where an assessment of longer-term trends is being sought. Not every crime or offence is detected; and even if the offender is detected, it may be impossible to bring it home to him. Statistics can give an indication only of recorded crime, and apparent trends may, for example, at any given time on examination be found to be attributable to changes in methods of detection, arrest and charging by the police, to changes in the law itself, or in the action of the courts, or even to side-effects of the statistics themselves. For example, if shoplifting appears to be on the increase, greater vigilance may well be exercised and possibly more shop detectives employed in large stores, and even more detections result. If more juvenile offenders are dealt with by police warning or by informal supervision, fewer juveniles may as a result appear before the courts. Again, public concern about certain types of crime may be reflected in an increased rate of police activity in respect of those crimes. Changing standards may result in some offences, e.g., fights involving youths, being prosecuted as more serious crimes involving bodily harm, which earlier might have been reported as simple assault, if reported at all. In Great Britain police strength between 1949 and 1959 rose by 20 per cent, and, after allowing for population changes, there were about 100 fewer persons to every policeman than 10 years previously; the police are backed by better and more scientific resources and communications, and are assisted by a greater number of civilian employees. These factors operate in various directions, but together they underline the need for caution in assessing the criminal statistics.

8. Appendix A shows that during the ten years 1950–1960, juvenile delinquency in Scotland showed a gradual decline during the mid-1950s, but thereafter it increased again, and by the end of the ten-year period was greater than in 1950. At the same time, until 1960 the increase does not appear to have done much more than keep pace with the increased child population. Despite the increase in crimes and offences, the annual rate remained fairly steadily between 2 and 2.5 per cent of the child population at risk. 1960 and later years appear to show signs of a different trend, but it is probably as yet too early to form any firm assessment. The figures suggest that, in relation to the total child population, juvenile delinquency in Scotland has remained over the post-war period at a surprisingly steady rate, which is not greatly in excess of the pre-war rate (1.8 per cent in 1938). Juvenile delinquents in fact still represent a very small minority within the child population as a whole, and it is clear that a very substantial proportion are brought before the courts for offences which must be reckoned on any objective criterion as in themselves trivial. By that we by no means imply any criticism of the action of the public agencies concerned. Such offences, which have all been under scrutiny both by senior police officers and public prosecutors before coming before the courts, are generally such as to justify public cognisance being taken of them. The major question fundamental to our inquiry is, of course, the form and machinery under which such cases should be made the subject of public action, and this we discuss in later chapters of this Report. What can be said is that this small minority of children who are offenders are, and must remain, a continuing source of public anxiety—because children's misdemeanours must naturally cause concern; because of the forms which such delinquency sometimes takes, and the worry, distress and loss which

in particular cases they may cause for the persons whose property is the subject of these attentions; and because they form a recruiting ground for the adult criminal. Moreover, if the field of juvenile delinquency is widened so as to include young adult offenders, i.e., those of 17–21, we find that about 28 per cent of all Scottish crimes and offences were committed by persons under 21— about 13 per cent by those under 17, and 15 per cent by those of 17–21. The latter group include in many cases young people who have had previous court appearances, and among the under-17s over 18 per cent had been the subject of a previous finding of guilt. (The latter figure is artificially low. Probation and absolute discharge do not technically result in a recording of guilt, and since the Criminal Statistics show only previous appearances resulting in a recording of guilt, this masks the fact that there is in reality an even higher proportion of previous appearances.)

Children in need of care or protection

9. The law recognises such children as a separate class. In such proceedings the child is not, of course, charged with any offence, and the procedure is essentially a civil one, although it may have criminal or quasi-criminal undertones—either in that it arises on a parent's conviction of child neglect, or because the facts or circumstances in question, while falling appreciably short of conduct justifying criminal sanctions, are of a kind which imply serious shortcomings on the part of the parents—shortcomings of such a nature as to justify the intervention of a court of law. Under existing law, children in need of care or protection are not a numerous class. We understand that in 1961–1962, 266 children were committed to the care of local authorities and 112 to approved schools on care or protection proceedings. Allowing for others who may have been committed to the care of other "fit persons" or placed under supervision, the annual total is probably not in excess of 500.

Refractory children beyond parental control

10. The figures mentioned in the previous paragraph include a small number of such cases. Circumstances justifying such action are clearly exceptional, and where they do arise are likely to call for careful inquiry into the home background and parental attitudes. Such cases are dealt with on what amount to "care or protection" proceedings. One of the questions discussed later in our Report is whether parents themselves should continue to be empowered to institute proceedings on such grounds.

Persistent truants

11. Truancy so persistent and serious as to justify court proceedings fortunately arises fairly rarely, and proceedings are likely to follow only where earlier discussions between parents and schools, and action by education committees, have failed. Truancy may be the product of a variety of causes, and may arise from maladjustment whether due to personal or environmental factors. Whatever action may be necessary, it will in almost all cases include treating the effects of some degree of educational retardment, and may thus often involve a period of residential school training. In 1961–62, 35 children were committed to Scottish approved schools on truancy proceedings. Here again, the proceedings are analogous to "care or protection" proceedings.

11

12. Any answer to the question—what is the best machinery for the treatment of juvenile delinquency—must reflect the acceptance of certain broad principles as to what are considered to be its essential function, since function affects both procedure and constitution. What then is the essential function? The object must be to effect, so far as this can be achieved by public action, the reduction, and ideally the elimination, of delinquency. If public concern must always be for the effective treatment of delinquency, the appropriate treatment measures in any individual case can be decided only on an informed assessment of the individual child's actual needs. Where the legal ground for public intervention has been established, this is the practical task to which the juvenile courts must address themselves in every case. This practical test—the needs of the individual child—is already recognised under statute inasmuch as the juvenile courts are required in every case to have regard to the welfare of the child and to secure proper provision for his education and training.

13. The children appearing before the juvenile courts do so for a variety of reasons, the circumstances in each case being such as to fulfil the criteria provided by one or other of the four legal classifications discussed in the preceding paragraphs. The great majority of the witnesses with whom we discussed this matter agreed, however, that in terms of the child's actual needs, the legal distinction between juvenile offenders and children in need of care or protection was—looking to the underlying realities—very often of little practical significance. At one extreme, there were cases in which children committed as being in need of care or protection were by reason of background and upbringing suffering from serious emotional disturbance. This found expression in conduct and behaviour which, while not resulting in criminal charges, clearly demanded sustained measures of education, training and discipline. The problems were of a degree and intensity calling for far more radical measures than in the case of many minor delinquencies committed by juvenile offenders. Equally, there were cases in which, where an offence had been committed by a child, no very drastic steps appeared to be justified on the basis of the offence itself. But these included cases in which, looking to the whole background, it might be that the child's quite minor delinquency was simply a symptom of personal or environmental difficulties, so that, for the prevention of more serious offences and for the future protection of society as much as in the child's own interests, more sustained measures of supervision were equally called for. From the standpoint of preventive measures, children in both groups could equally be said to be in need of special measures of education and training—"education" being taken in its widest sense. The emphasis in these training measures might vary according to the circumstances of the individual case; in some the protection of the child would be of prime importance, in others the training regime might place more emphasis on discipline. Each case had, however, to be assessed on its merits, and the type of training, whether stressing the protective aspect, the disciplinary, or for that matter the need for special instruction in formal educational subjects on account of educational backwardness, had no necessary connection with the legal classification of children as delinquents or as children in need of care or protection.

14. The same is true of children brought before the courts as persistent truants or as beyond parental control. In the experience of the witnesses, persistent truancy is in many cases a manifestation of emotional disturbance often

attributable to factors in the home and family background. So also the fact that a child is so refractory as to be beyond parental control calls in all cases for careful enquiry into the home and family circumstances and is likely to be attributable to factors personal to the child or to the parents themselves.

15. The consensus of experienced opinion which emerged from our discussions was that, for the purposes of treatment measures, these various classifications could not in practice be usefully considered as presenting a series of distinct and separately definable problems, calling in turn for distinct and separate principles of treatment. The basic similarity of underlying situation far outweighs the differences, and from the point of view of treatment measures the true distinguishing factor, common to all the children concerned, is their need for special measures of education and training, the normal up-bringing processes having, for whatever reason, fallen short. Against that background, we have had to consider how far the present treatment measures, as available and as applied, can be said to fulfil the criterion of actual need as revealed in our discussions.

THE EFFECTIVENESS OF THE PRESENT TREATMENT MEASURE:
VIEWS OF WITNESSES

16. We received various suggestions for changes in the detailed arrangements governing some of the existing forms of treatment. These, however, implied the broad acceptance of the underlying soundness of these methods, and over the entire field, we received, with few exceptions, little positive evidence as to their general effectiveness or otherwise. This is, of course, in no sense a criticism of the witnesses. The fact is that in these matters there is a practically unlimited and as yet almost untouched field for systematic study and research. Even were systematic information of this kind available on a far greater scale than at present, it could never amount to more than a body of valuable general information, whose successful application to the severely practical daily task of adjudication, in children's problems especially, calls for a high degree of skill and discrimination, and for special qualities of insight and understanding. Nevertheless, the test of any treatment measures must ultimately be the practical one of their apparent effectiveness or otherwise, and the general tenor of much of the evidence before us indicated a fairly strong, though not always fully articulate, sense of dissatisfaction and unease on this score.

17. In the main, the existing arrangements for the treatment of juvenile delinquency appear to be based on what is essentially an educational principle, in that they seek to apply measures of social education, in the great majority of cases carried on while the child remains within the home, but which may also sometimes involve his removal for temporary periods for more specialised and intensive residential training. The underlying aim of all such measures must always be, wherever possible, to strengthen and further those natural influences for good which will assist the child's development into a mature and useful member of society. The most powerful and direct of these influences lies in the home—and in almost all cases, however the measures applied are expressed as a matter of formal or legal terminology, they must necessarily imply working in the closest co-operation with the parents. This ought to be so not only where the child is subject to special measures within the community (i.e., while normally continuing to live at home), but equally where he has to be removed from home for residential training. It is, we think, necessary to stress this. While the

13

importance of parental influence on the child is universally accepted, the conclusion sometimes drawn is that action needs to be directed as much (if not more so) against the parents as the child.

18. The latter view often finds practical expression in proposals for (*a*) the greater use of fines (and an increase in the financial limits of fining powers) against parents for the misdemeanours of their children, (*b*) requiring parents to make financial restitution for damage caused as a result of their children's delinquent behaviour, and (*c*) the placing of parents directly under compulsory measures of supervision in consequence of their children's misdemeanours. Proposals on these lines were put before us by several witnesses, though we think it fair to say in most cases on a tentative basis and recognising that they were not free from serious difficulties both of principle and practice. All of these proposals stem, as we have said, from a recognition of the importance of parental influence and attitudes in the child's up-bringing. They are aimed at bringing home to parents their responsibilities; and by that means strengthening and furthering those natural instincts for the good of the child which are common to parents, even though in particular cases these may be temporarily latent or overlaid by extraneous factors.

PARENTAL RESPONSIBILITY AND HOW IT CAN BE FURTHERED

19. We have found great difficulty in reconciling such proposals with their declared aims. Under existing arrangements criminal sanctions can be applied against adult persons only in carefully defined situations amounting to the commission of crimes or offences. Where the adult is also a parent, criminal sanctions relating to matters within the home can arise only in the most extreme situations amounting to either to criminal neglect or to the commission of unnatural offences against the children. We recognise that there may be a variety of situations falling short of the stringent standard of criminal neglect in the legal sense, in which children may be the sufferers and in which there may equally be present many of the factors of incipient delinquency (in some cases leading to the actual commission of acts of juvenile delinquency). Such situations are, however, scarcely capable of being stated in a form which would ever be appropriate to the criminal law. With hindsight one can say that such and such a parental failure contributed to this child's delinquency; it is an entirely different matter, with different children all with different needs, to attempt to state parental duties in such a form that criminal sanctions might be applied. In a free society, we do not consider that proposals for so sweeping an extension of coercive powers against adult persons—on the basis of facts and circumstances failing far short of any existing standard of criminal neglect or criminal misconduct—could ever be tolerated as a result of proceedings instituted in a juvenile court ostensibly concerned with the child's delinquency, or, in some cases, incipient delinquent tendencies.

Supervision of parents

20. It seems to us that society has for long taken the view—

(*a*) that adults are in general to be regarded as responsible agents, and that, however limited the practical range of choices open to them, they are free agents:

14

(*b*)   that this does not, however, apply universally, and various classes, e.g., children, do not enjoy the same rights and privileges, nor are they in consequence subject to the same duties;

(*c*)   that equally it is impossible in practice to trace a direct responsibility for one person's acts to another, even where the individuals concerned are parent and child.

On the propositions stated, the application of coercive measures by way of supervision directly on the parents seems to us untenable. Under the guise of promoting the welfare of the child, such proposals appear to be in risk of ending in the application of coercive measures against the parents on the basis of a somewhat vaguely-defined aim of improving the quality of family life; and of assuming a prescriptive right not merely to try to prevent juvenile delinquency but to improve, by direct coercive measures, adult people—on the footing that there is a duty in the State to promote universal happiness among its citizens.

21.   These arguments do not in any way detract from the usefulness, as a practical basis of approach to the problem of juvenile delinquency, of regarding the child as an individual within a system of family relationships in a particular context. Indeed, in practice, all social case-work proceeds on the basis of persuasion and co-operation; and presupposes that the individual is to be regarded as a free agent, who on a fuller insight into the nature of his problems and responsibilities, is capable of a voluntary response, however halting, and that indeed change can be brought about successfully only if there is such a response. Within the widely varying scale of growing responsibility in children this factor will also be present. The child's response can in many cases be appreciably influenced by parental attitudes. So far as case-work in relation to the parents is concerned, however, since ultimately the whole basis must be persuasive and co-operative, it is difficult to see what further useful results could be obtained in such circumstances by placing the parents directly under supervision; and assuming they were, how as a practical matter—short of evidence sufficient to justify a criminal charge of neglect—they could ever be adjudged to be culpably in default to a degree justifying further sanctions (which other than financial could probably not amount to anything other than imprisonment). Compulsory supervision of the child can, and often will, take the shape of family case-work; when it does, it can be a highly beneficial process. Its basic approach is, however, utterly different from one implying compulsory measures on the parents directly.

22.   If for these reasons, we must reject proposals for placing parents under supervision, equally the practice of fining parents for their children's misdemeanours seems to be open to serious objection. As a simple, expeditious measure not involving continued demands on the parent or intrusion into the home it may be felt to commend itself. In principle, however, it seems to us equally incompatible with what purports to be a system of measures for the education and training of children. Fining of parents is essentially a punitive measure, and, while we certainly do not wish to suggest that punishment as applied to children themselves has never any educational value, the fact is that fining in these circumstances amounts to a vicarious liability on the parents, who are punished (by financial deprivation) for acts committed by their children. The educational value, in relation to the parents, must in the circumstances be highly doubtful; and the argument that the process win indirectly be of educational value to the child we consider to be untenable.

Fines on parents

23.   The practical difficulty, to which we have already referred, of establishing convincingly in a particular situation a direct relationship between general parental attitudes and specific acts committed by the child, has, of course, been recognised under existing law governing the imposition of fines in such circumstances. Under Section 59 of the 1937 Act, if the juvenile offender is a child, any fine imposed must be on the parent, unless the court is satisfied that the parent cannot be found or that he has not conduced to the commission of the offence by neglecting to exercise due care of the child. In the case of a young person, a fine may be imposed either on him or his parents, but in ordering a fine to be paid by the parent, the court has to be satisfied on the same considerations as to failure to exercise due care.

24.   Prior to the passing of the Children Act, 1908, it seems doubtful whether the question of fining juvenile offenders arose to any extent. In earlier times juveniles were for the purpose of criminal proceedings treated in the same way as adults. While thus in theory liable to the same penalties as adults, given the economic and financial conditions then prevailing it is doubtful whether the penalty of fining (as distinct from other sanctions) was in practice applied to any great extent. In so far as it was applied, the fine would be likely to be imposed on the juvenile directly and not on the parent. Moreover, there have always, under Scots law, been strict limitations on parental liability in civil law for the delictal acts of minors.

25.   Section 59 of the 1937 Act was in fact a re-enactment of a provision of the Children Act, 1908 (a Great Britain measure); and so far as fines are concerned, it therefore appears that in Scotland the present position in relation to juveniles is of fairly recent statutory origin, and that, in so far as it imports the idea of applying, subject to certain qualifications, penalties on the parents for the misdeeds of their children, it represents a concept not otherwise found in the criminal law, or to any appreciable extent in the civil law. The effect of the 1937 Act is to create a rebuttable presumption—the onus being on the parent (not the court) to show that he did not fail to exercise due care of the child or young person. In other words, it is not necessary for the court to be satisfied affirmatively that the parent has conduced to the commission of the offence; and in practice courts are no doubt guided, in the absence of any positive attempt at rebuttal by the parents, by the background report and other information before them, and by the parents' general demeanour on appearance before them.

26.   The report of the earlier Departmental Committee on "Protection and Training"* suggested that the effect of the provision (now re-enacted in the 1937 Act) was misunderstood in some juvenile courts, which tended to assume that the onus rested on the prosecution to prove that the parent or guardian had conduced to the commission of the offence—before a fine could be imposed— and, in their words, "this proof is almost impossible to obtain". Because of this misunderstanding of the provisions of the Act, and the fact that at that time imposition of a fine resulted in a conviction being recorded against the child, the Committee felt that the provision was not as widely used as it might be, and they expressed the hope that their comments and recommendations would lead to greater use of fines. In 1925, the number of fines imposed by juvenile courts was 3,182.

---

* "Protection and Training": Report of Departmental Committee, 1928

27.   While such research studies as have been made of the effectiveness of different methods of treatment are necessarily subject to qualification, there is reason to think (e.g., from the study appended to Report, by the Scottish Advisory Council on the Treatment of Offenders, on " Short Sentences of Imprisonment"*) that fining is on the whole not an ineffective method of treatment in relation to wage-earners, and it may be in modern economic conditions that a financial penalty will in many cases be particularly effective. This can, however, scarcely apply to children of school age who are with few exceptions not wage-earners; and for the reasons indicated above, it seems to us doubtful whether fining of parents is an appropriate or effective method of dealing with juvenile offenders. If, as the Committee on "Protection and Training" argued, it is impracticable to place an onus on the court to be satisfied that parents have failed to exercise due care and control, it is equally difficult to see how, on the basis of the present rebuttable presumption, in many cases the parents, however well-meaning, can be expected to discharge the onus of satisfying the court that they did not in fact fail to exercise due care of their children. Cases can readily be cited of apparently wanton damage to costly public installations by young children; but, in many populous areas, it seems doubtful whether in such circumstances there can be said to be in any definable sense a failure of parental control. The streets are to some extent the playgrounds, and public installations have natural attractions. This by no means implies that the children in question are not in need of some kind of lesson, but in such circumstances it seems questionable whether fining the parents is likely to be an effective remedy.

28.   In 1962, 8,428 fines were imposed in respect of juveniles under 17, of which 5,788 were imposed on children under 16. Of the latter figure 5,042 were imposed on the child, and the remainder on the parent or guardian. Most of these fines were, we assume, in fact paid by the parents, the alternative (where imposed on the child) in event of default being the child's detention in a remand home. We cannot regard either of these results as being satisfactory either as an effective measure of training for the child or as being likely to secure genuine parental co-operation. The situation seems to us to be quite different in the case of young people beyond school-leaving age, and in 1962, of the 2,640 fines imposed in such cases all but 26 were imposed directly on the young person.

29.   At present a fair number of minor offences (more especially involving road traffic and "municipal" offences) committed by juveniles are dealt with by fines. No very complicated or sustained measures may be necessary in many such cases; if so, it seems to us that, in the case of non-wage-earners, they could more appropriately and effectively be dealt with by other means. It is generally recognised that many children nowadays receive substantial pocket-money, and where fines are imposed, courts frequently offer exhortations to parents to stop a child's pocket-money in whole or in part towards meeting the cost of the fine. This is no doubt sometimes a useful practice as a matter of exhortation; it is not one which could, we suggest, be a matter for statutory provision.

Restitution by parents
30.   Under existing law, the juvenile courts have no power to order the payment of the cost of damage resulting from acts done by juvenile offenders. The

---

* "Short Sentences of Imprisonment": Report by the Scottish Advisory Council on the Treatment of Offenders, 1960.

statutory provision in the Children Act, 1908 (a Great Britain measure) which formerly enabled them to do so was (like other provisions relating to orders for restitution by the criminal courts) repealed by the Criminal Justice (Scotland) Act, 1949, on the ground that these were not matters appropriate to the criminal courts. We do not propose that there should be provision for the making of such orders against children, inasmuch as children are not to any appreciable extent wage-earners and cannot be expected to make financial recompense. In discussions before us, however, the idea of restitution by the child was sometimes expressed in rather wider terms implying that he might on occasion be required to make indirect restitution through, for example, attendance at some specified centre where he would be required to undertake certain prescribed, and socially useful, tasks. While such a concept is not without value, it is, we think, extremely difficult to translate into practical terms which could find expression as a statutory measure of treatment. Equally, the widely varying capacity and understanding of children at various ages makes it difficult to ensure that more indirect measures of this kind would be seen clearly by the child to have any element of recompense for those who have suffered loss or serious inconvenience from his actions. In saying this, we do not rule out the idea of the child's attendance at a specified centre as an appropriate method of treatment in certain cases, but we doubt whether such an arrangement would in fact convey any idea of restitution to the child. In so far as it involved loss of leisure for him, it would be seen simply as a punishment; if it involved useful social training, this would not be likely to be regarded by the child as an act of restitution.

31.　Restitution, not by the child, but by his parents, is, however, not uncommonly advocated. As regards the liability of a parent to make restitution for damage caused by his child, the civil law in fact entertains such claims only in very restricted circumstances, and it may thus be helpful to set out at some length the present civil law principles governing parental liability in this field. This is done in Appendix B. At the present stage it is, however, sufficient to say that the essential principle of Scots law is that a parent is not liable in respect of damage caused by his child unless he himself has been at fault. Actions against parents for the wrongful acts of their children (to the very limited extent recognised under the civil law) raise legal questions arising on claims which are essentially matters for adjudication in the civil courts of law.

32.　The question of civil actions apart, we are of opinion that it would be inappropriate, as part of the treatment measures to be applied in respect of the delinquent child, to introduce a statutory power to order the payment by parents of the cost of repairing damage done by their children. As we have already indicated, such a proposal seems to us to assume a directness of relationship between a parent's actions and the individual actions of the child which could hardly ever be established. Where the child's actions had been committed spontaneously, it would also be well-nigh impossible to establish convincingly that there had been a failure of parental control. While the actual damage done is often extensive in financial terms, the objects concerned are very often to be found in places to which children have the readiest access and of whose value they have no real understanding. Even if in many cases the background circumstances are such as to create a presumption that there is in a general way a lack of parental guidance, it would equally be necessary to consider how far this may be attributable either to external circumstances or to constitutional

18

defects personal to the parents. The effect of such factors can in many cases be mitigated with the skilled help and guidance of trained social workers, but it seems extremely doubtful whether—assuming such measures were adopted—the simultaneous application, on a compulsive basis, of financial sanctions in the form of restitution would be beneficial as an educational process; they would be likely to be even less intelligible to the child. Restitution on this basis would, we think, in many cases be seen as simply a financial sanction virtually indistinguishable from a fine—imposed in circumstances in which the parent would frequently be quite unable to regard the acts in question as arising in any definable sense from a lack of parental control on his part.

33.   Restitution on a voluntary basis, arrived at with the agreement of parents, seems to us on the other hand to be highly desirable, and the present practice in some areas of inviting the co-operation of parents in this way is to be commended and encouraged.

Corporal punishment

34.   In reviewing the suggestions brought before us, it is convenient to refer at this point to corporal punishment as a public measure for the treatment of juvenile delinquency. Few of the witnesses who submitted evidence to us offered any comment on this subject, and the few who did so were divided—those in favour of its reintroduction making clear that they contemplated its limitation to younger children who had committed relatively minor delinquent acts for which no sustained measures were necessary. The imposition of corporal punishment as a public treatment measure raises issues entirely separate from those relating to its use in the home or in schools. Its employment as a public treatment measure, even in the limited form suggested, inevitably raises serious practical questions both as to its efficacy and as to the agency which might be made responsible for its administration. Prompt action taken by parents for their children's misdemeanours may be both readily intelligible and salutary to the child. Similar action at the instance of a public agency, with the element of delay necessarily resulting, seems unlikely to be either efficacious or often readily comprehensible to the child. Even assuming that such action were felt to be appropriate in principle, we strongly doubt whether either the police or any of the existing social services would willingly undertake the task of administering corporal punishment ordered as a public treatment measure. More important, however, it seems to us that such proposals represent a negation of parental responsibility, since they assume a degree of parental failure or of lack of parental willingness to co-operate in the child's education such as to justify public intervention. That intervention would, however, on the proposals discussed, take a form which from its nature scarcely implied so serious an assessment of the underlying situation. The educational effect, whether in relation to parent or child, must in such circumstances be extremely doubtful, and public intervention between parent and child, if justified, should clearly be carried out in a manner which is likely to be effective. None of the witnesses who commented on the matter was able to offer any evidence of the effectiveness of such action in the past, and for our part we are unable to accept that corporal punishment of children can appropriately form part of the range of public treatment measures.

35.   The principle underlying the present range of treatment measures is, as we have indicated, primarily an educational one, in the sense that it is intended, wherever possible, not to supersede the natural beneficial influences of the home and the family, but wherever practicable to strengthen, support and supplement them in situations in which for whatever reason they have been weakened or have failed in their effect. Proposals for a more sweeping extension of coercive powers in relation to parents of juvenile delinquents are in our view not only unacceptable on general grounds (as implying the application of criminal sanctions against adult persons in circumstances in which no definable criminal offence has been committed); but are ultimately incompatible with the nature of educational process itself, more particularly in the context of the parent–child relationship. Such a process of education in a social context—or "social education" as we now describe it—essentially involves the application of social and family case-work. In practice, this can work only on a persuasive and co-operative basis, through which the individual parent and child can be assisted towards a fuller insight and understanding of their situation and problems, and the means of solution which lie to their hands. There is, we consider, already ample evidence that, to the extent that it is already applied, such an approach finds a ready response. This is especially so with parents, enlisting as it does their active commitment as participants in a process which for their part they are increasingly led to see as being in the true interests of their children. Such an approach seems to us to be a proper and appropriate one for the solution of the problems of the child within the family. Indeed, we consider that the alternative already discussed, based as it is on the view that in matters so closely concerning their children the co-operation of parents as adult persons can be enlisted by compulsory sanctions, is fundamentally misconceived and unlikely to lead to any practical and beneficial result.

36.   If then the existing arrangements are nevertheless unsatisfactory, this does not seem to us to point to some new and totally different basis of approach, but rather to a consideration of the points at which the present machinery fails to give full effect to the educational principle on which the existing treatment measures in general purport to be based. If the conclusion which emerged from the evidence before us was that the better up-bringing of their children cannot be secured by compulsory sanctions on parents, we were also convinced that in various directions the present arrangements do not go far enough in enlisting the co-operation of parents and in some situations appear positively to militate against it. Fining of parents may, on the arguments already discussed, work against parental co-operation in this way. Other examples brought to our notice relate to the nature of proceedings in the juvenile court itself, and to the high proportion of cases dealt with there by absolute discharge or admonition. The proceedings are, by their nature, primarily directed towards the child himself; but section 42 of the Children and Young Persons (Scotland) Act, 1937, requires that, with certain exceptions, one of the parents must be present, and empowers the court, in any case, to order the presence of both parents. (We understand that this latter power is seldom used.) From our experience we are satisfied that the present procedures fall far short of what is desirable in obtaining parental co-operation. We accept that many juvenile courts are overworked—a situation for which society itself must bear responsibility, but, that apart, the parent who accompanies the child very frequently makes a "plea in mitigation" for the child, a plea that the offence should be regarded as an isolated piece of juvenile

mischief; and we think that few courts can, or do, spend time in persuading parents to face the potential seriousness of the situation or in obtaining their co-operation in the necessary treatment measures. Unless probation or some other form of formal supervision ensues, there is little opportunity for sustained action to obtain parental co-operation at the outset.

37.   In fact, 37.3 per cent of disposals by juvenile courts in 1962 took the form of absolute discharge or admonition. This may be an accurate pointer to the relative triviality of a large proportion of juvenile offences viewed as such. On the assumption that admonition or absolute discharge was the best available disposal, doubts arise whether in all such cases court appearance was strictly necessary. We recognise that there may be cases in which a warning seems the appropriate outcome, and that appearance before a court may itself sometimes be considered to have a salutary effect. In many other cases the educational effect of warnings given in the circumstances of a criminal court—whether in relation to parent or child—seems to be seriously in doubt. Equally, the high proportion of admonitions and absolute discharges leaves a doubt whether, in some cases at least, background features are fully taken into account; and it may be that as a result some cases are in effect being dismissed where there is in fact a need (whether or not by formal supervision) to enlist the parents' active co-operation and support in the education of the child.

38.   Further, where the child's removal from home for residential training has to be ordered, the result in many cases at present cannot, it was suggested to us, fail to appear to the parents as extinguishing their responsibility. With the child's removal from the scene they are still too often left largely to their own devices; and, while it is accepted that in most cases the child must eventually return to the home, official contact where maintained with the parents tends at best to be tenuous and intermittent. In such circumstances it is in many cases almost impossible, in the absence of any really close continuing relationship with the parents, to assist them to any informed understanding of the processes at work for their child; to persuade them that they have any immediate or future part in them; or to assist them in making the personal adjustments necessary either to overcome those factors, personal or external, which led to the child's removal, or which in the changed situation will equally be necessary if he is to settle down satisfactorily on his eventual return. It was represented to us that too often the results of the present arrangements may in this respect appear to amount to a process of shuffling from one agency to another, in which at various transient points in time the intervention of the courts is momentarily invoked. At no stage can there be said to be any clear sense of comprehensive direction; no single agency being specifically charged with a definite, inescapable and continuing responsibility for the child's training needs; and the parents for their part being reduced to the role of passive spectators.

39.   In the light of these criticisms, it would appear that, if the concept of educational process were to be fully accepted, this would entail nothing less than the formation in every area of a locally-based treatment authority, recognised as having specific responsibility for the prevention and reduction of juvenile delinquency; either having under its direct control or having a recognised right of access to all those local social services (public and voluntary) primarily concerned with children's problems; having a direct and continuous responsibility for the children within its jurisdiction; and affording

the fullest scope for enlisting the parents' co-operation and support in the measures to be applied at all stages. In the next Chapters, we examine more fully, first, how far the present arrangements meet these criteria; how far such shortcomings as may exist are attributable to mere defects of machinery or are fundamental to the whole basis of the present scheme of juvenile courts; and in the light of such an examination, what appear to us to be the practical alternatives confronting society at the present time.

CHAPTER II

The Juvenile Courts—The Existing Arrangements

BACKGROUND TO THE EXISTING ARRANGEMENTS

40.   Under the common law, no child under the age of 7 could be charged with a criminal offence. Beyond that age children were assumed to be criminally responsible, though the element of youth was recognised as a mitigating factor in relation to punishment. The principle that the hearing of cases involving juveniles raises special considerations and that juvenile offenders should receive different treatment from adults seems to have been implicitly recognised from very early times, though it may largely have been lost sight of at various periods. In the first half of the nineteenth century, the harshness of the penal code and the social conditions following the Industrial Revolution led to many young offenders being sentenced to imprisonment or transportation. Public opinion reacted increasingly against such methods of punishment of the young, and consequent reforms helped to mitigate the severity of the law—notably through the evolution of reformatory or industrial schools as alternatives to prison, the trial of children summarily for most offences, and the development of what is now the probation system.

41.   The Children Act, 1908—which applied to England and Scotland alike—was a major landmark, in that it established certain principles which continue to govern the operation of the juvenile courts today, later legislation being more in the direction of amplifying and expanding the detailed arrangements rather than introducing any new basis of approach. The 1908 Act proceeded on the footing that young offenders should be treated differently from adults, and that the aim should be to seek to educate and reform, rather than to punish. Courts of summary jurisdiction when hearing charges against children and young persons were to sit either in a different building or room from that in which the ordinary sittings of the court were held, or on different days or at different times from those at which the ordinary sittings took place. Proceedings were to be in private, and special provision was made for the segregation of juveniles and adults during the hearings.

42.   In 1925 a Scottish departmental committee, under the chairmanship of Sir George Morton, K.C., was appointed to enquire into the treatment of young offenders and young people requiring care or protection. The Committee* found that throughout Scotland the general pattern was for juvenile cases to be heard

---

* Report of the Departmental Committee. "Protection and Training", 1928.

by the Sheriff Courts or the Burgh Courts, and that, except in Lanarkshire, juvenile courts attached to the Justice of the Peace Courts were not functioning to any extent. The Committee recommended transfer of jurisdiction in the case of children and young offenders to specially constituted Justice of the Peace juvenile courts—the members of the court to be drawn from a panel of justices, appointed by the body of justices as a whole from their own number, and comprising persons who by knowledge and experience were specially qualified to consider juvenile cases. The Children and Young Persons (Scotland) Act, 1932 (later consolidated in the Children and Young Persons (Scotland) Act, 1937), provided for the setting up of such courts in any area where an order to that effect has been made by the Secretary of State. Only four such orders have been made—all prior to 1940—applying to the counties of Ayr, Fife, Renfrew and the city of Aberdeen. A further recommendation of the 1925 Committee— for the raising of the minimum age of criminal responsibility from 7 to 8 years of age—was also enacted in 1932.

The Existing Juvenile Courts

43.   We were thus faced at the outset of our inquiry with the fact that throughout Scotland four distinct types of court are at present dealing with juvenile cases, namely, the Sheriff Court, the Burgh (or Police) Courts, the Justice of the Peace Courts, and—in Ayrshire, Renfrewshire, Fife and the city of Aberdeen—the specially constituted J.P. Juvenile Courts. The Sheriff Juvenile Court is, of course, presided over by a single judge (normally a Sheriff-Substitute) who is legally qualified and whose appointment is permanent. The Burgh (or Police) Courts on the other hand are presided over by a single bailie, who holds office normally for three years, and is an elected town councillor appointed to this office by his fellow councillors. Justice of the Peace Courts comprise lay justices from the roll of justices appointed to the Commission of the Peace on the nomination of the Secretary of State, appointments being permanent, subject only to an upper age-limit. In the four areas having specially constituted J.P. Juvenile Courts, the special panel of justices for this purpose is appointed by the body of Justices from their own number for a period of three years, appointments being renewable and subject to a retiring age-limit of 65. In the city of Glasgow the work of the Police Courts is spread among three courts (the Central, Marine and Govan Police Courts). The former is presided over by the Stipendiary Magistrate, who is legally qualified and holds full-time appointment, while the two latter are presided over by bailies. These three courts, which sit as courts of summary jurisdiction dealing with adult offenders in the city, also sit as juvenile courts.

Choice of Court in Individual Cases

44.   In relation to individual cases, the choice of court may be affected by the following considerations. First, the Summary Jurisdiction (Scotland) Act, 1954, provides that various common law offences, principally those involving dishonesty (theft, fraud, etc.) in which the value of the stolen goods exceeds a certain figure, are not to be taken in burgh or J.P. courts but in the Sheriff Court, and outside the four areas with special J.P. Juvenile Courts, this has the effect that an appreciable number of juvenile cases are heard in the Sheriff Court (sitting as a juvenile court). Secondly, in many landward areas, J.P. courts do not function, or function only rarely, and in practice in these areas all juvenile cases

are heard by the Sheriff Court since it is functioning permanently. Thirdly, while the 1937 Act proceeds on the general assumption that juvenile cases will be heard summarily, this is subject to the over-riding discretion of the Lord Advocate under the common law to direct the taking of particular cases in the Sheriff Court or a higher court, either summarily or on indictment. Fourthly, while the specially constituted J.P. Juvenile Courts in the four areas mentioned have the same jurisdiction to hear juvenile cases as the Sheriff Court, and their powers are in practice similar (except in relation to the power to order borstal training), the Act expressly saves the power of the Lord Advocate to order proceedings to be taken in the Sheriff Court or the High Court. Moreover, it was held in *Weir* v. *Cruickshank* (1959, J.C. 94) that in these areas the Sheriff Court retains a concurrent jurisdiction with the special J.P. Juvenile Court. Fifthly, we understand that in view of doubts as to the power of courts of summary jurisdiction (other than the Sheriff Court) to order disqualification on conviction of road traffic offences, it has hitherto been the general practice to take juvenile cases involving offences carrying such a liability in the Sheriff Court. (Under the Road Traffic Act, 1962, the Sheriff Court is now the sole court of summary jurisdiction with power to order disqualification.)

DISTRIBUTION OF JUVENILE COURT BUSINESS

45. All these factors influence the distribution of business in the juvenile courts, which in 1962 was broadly as follows:

Sheriff Courts—32 per cent;

Burgh (Police) Courts—45 per cent (the Glasgow Police Courts accounting for about 33 per cent);

Specially constituted J.P. Juvenile Courts—16 per cent;

Other J.P. Courts—7 per cent.

THE NON-CRIMINAL JURISDICTION OF THE JUVENILE COURTS

46. All juvenile courts, in addition to exercising a criminal jurisdiction in respect of juvenile offenders, have a civil or protective jurisdiction in relation to "care or protection" cases (including truancy and refractory cases beyond parental control), though as the figures indicate, these occupy only a small proportion of the courts' time. In most areas, the same juvenile court deals with juvenile offenders and juveniles in need of care or protection alike. In Edinburgh, however, the Burgh Juvenile Court does not deal with truancy cases, or in Glasgow with care or protection proceedings (including truancy cases). These are in both cities dealt with by the J.P. Juvenile Courts, or, in some cases, by the Sheriff Juvenile Courts.

VARIETY OF JUVENILE COURTS—
PRELIMINARY OBSERVATIONS ON THE EVIDENCE RECEIVED

47. These local arrangements rest in many cases simply on practice and have no doubt been developed in response to the needs of particular local situations rather than on any consciously-aimed principle. It is, however, clear that— the four special areas apart—the Justice of the Peace Courts in Scotland play only a limited part in the hearing of juvenile cases, that in this field, as in criminal cases generally, even allowing for the special juvenile courts in the four areas, the J.P. Court has not taken extensive root in Scotland, and that in this respect the situation is very different from that prevailing in England and Wales.

24

48.   Faced with this variety of juvenile courts, a number of the witnesses who appeared before us urged the adoption of a uniform system, or, short of that, a reduction in the number of existing types of juvenile court. Contrast was drawn, at one level of discussion, between the characteristics of each of the main types of court, it being said, for example, that the hearing of juvenile cases demanded special knowledge, experience and sympathetic understanding of children— qualities not necessarily to be found among those presiding in the Sheriff or Burgh Courts, though within both it was no doubt possible to point to individual persons who admirably fulfilled this criterion. It was equally conceded that while the Juvenile Court Rules governing the appointment of panels for the specially constituted J.P. Juvenile Courts assumed that those concerned were to be "specially qualified," there was no clear criterion as to qualifications; that in fact in some areas such appointments (made by the Justices from their own number) tended to be on a somewhat arbitrary basis; and that even in these areas there was sometimes very little continuity of service on the juvenile court bench. On the other hand, in support of the burgh courts, it was said that the magistrates usually had a reasonably intimate practical knowledge of local social conditions and great familiarity with the local idiom, and might in that sense be expected to establish closer contact with the children appearing before them. It was, however, recognised that local knowledge was not in itself a sufficient criterion, that the qualities to be looked for were essentially personal, and could not be guaranteed by the present or any other preconceived arrangement.

49.   Those of our witnesses who were concerned about the effects of lack of continuity tended to assume that a preferable solution might lie in the transfer of all juvenile court business to the Sheriff Courts, and some visualised that in such a situation the Sheriff-Substitute might sit with lay assessors, a hybrid bench of this kind combining the advantages of legal training (of advantage in relation to the determination of innocence or guilt) and of special qualities of experience and understanding of children (of special value in considering the methods of treatment to be applied). We do not consider it necessary at this stage to comment in detail on the various arguments, save to indicate that they point to two separate aspects of court procedure, namely, the legal issue of determination of guilt or innocence; and, in cases in which there is a finding of guilt, the subsequent question of sentence, or measures to be applied appropriate to the circumstances of the case.

CHAPTER III

The Underlying Principles

CONCEPTS UNDERLYING THE JUVENILE COURT

50. The existing juvenile courts, despite their differences of personnel and organisation, form part of the system of courts of summary jurisdiction, i.e., all are courts of criminal law. The essence of this system lies in the following sequence of events. A criminal prosecution is instituted: either there is an admission of guilt by the accused or a finding of guilt or innocence after trial, and where guilt is established the court passes sentence. It is true that, under the Juvenile Court Rules, the juvenile court procedure is modified in certain respects in the interests of simplicity and intelligibility for the juvenile, but this does not represent any fundamental alteration in the principles of criminal procedure. It is true that once guilt is established, the juvenile court does not proceed to a conviction, but records a "finding of guilt", except where a probation order or order of absolute discharge is made—in which case no finding of guilt is recorded. These are, however, differences of nomenclature rather than of fact. Moreover, most of the court's orders apply, with modifications on account of age, the forms of sentence which may be passed by a criminal court on an adult. Criminal procedure in the sense described is clearly well-adapted to determination of questions of fact, from which the accused's innocence or guilt may be inferred. By its nature it focuses attention on the specific act alleged, which, if proved, constitutes a crime or offence. In relation to juvenile offenders, however, statute law introduces a further set of considerations. A court in dealing with a juvenile is required to have regard to the welfare of the person before it. "Welfare" is, of course, irrelevant to the question of determination of innocence or guilt, and relates to the second stage of the proceedings, namely, the form of treatment appropriate to the case once the facts alleged have been proved.

51. It is evident that the system of criminal prosecution assumes a high degree of personal responsibility—of choice in doing right or wrong, and that doing wrong—where this involves the commission of an act recognised by law as a criminal offence—merits punishment. In the ultimate, this might seem to imply that every crime detected ought to be followed by criminal proceedings so that the offender can receive the punishment he deserves. Although in practice this consequence does not invariably follow, it is the case that, where prosecution does follow, the possible legal consequences demand the most stringent safeguards to ensure that the innocent are not punished. The law provides these safeguards for the protection of the accused, and the prosecutor must undertake the whole burden of proving the guilt of the accused beyond reasonable doubt by competent evidence.

52. The court's first function is thus the determination of guilt or innocence, and where it convicts, its further function is then to determine, after taking account of any mitigating circumstances, the appropriate punishment. The first determination depends on evidence of facts (i.e. past events) which are sufficient to support a judicial finding of guilt, and the acquittal of the accused if that evidence is deficient. The second of the court's functions—that of sentencing—has, certainly in more recent times, increasingly had regard not simply to fitting

the punishment to the crime, but to the future. Sentencing looks to the future in that considerations of deterrence are or may be present, both in relation to the offender and to others, and in that the principle of educating and reforming the criminal has in more modern times received increasing attention.

53.　If the underlying principle were simply the prevention of crime at all costs, and this were to accepted in pure form, a very different scheme would be necessary. Since the criterion would be simply the protection of society, primary concern would then rest in the prevention of future criminal actions by the treatment of all the factors, whether personal or environmental, likely to conduce to such actions by a person who, either because he has already offended or on some other evidence, has shown himself prone to delinquency. Punishment need not be alien to such a concept, since punishment might be good treatment for the particular person concerned in his particular circumstances: but punishment would be imposed for its value to the purpose of treatment, not for its own sake as some sort of reward for ill-doing.

54.　In drawing a contrast between a system resting primarily on ideas of crime, responsibility and punishment and one proceeding primarily on the principle of prevention, we are not, of course, suggesting that the methods of dealing with adult crime are entirely governed by the first concept or that a working compromise between them is not possible. In practice the present arrangements represent such a compromise, and, at any given time and certainly in relation to any individual offender, a balance has to be sought on an empirical basis between the conflicting claims of the two principles. While, however, compromise on such a basis is possible, it seems to us important to indicate points at which the two concepts are incompatible or militate against each other—

(1) *Early preventive measures*: the "crime–responsibility–punishment" concept militates against preventive action against potential delinquents. Because of the high degree of personal responsibility which it attaches to the criminal, a stigma is attached in the public eye to conviction of a crime, which bears no necessary relationship to the harm done by the action itself or the actual responsibility of the person who did it. Because it is concerned with the deserts of a criminal, the standard of proof is high. In the absence of such proof—even though it is clear that the surrounding circumstances are such as to call urgently for preventive action—no such action can be taken since it would involve treating as criminals persons who have not been convicted by a criminal court.

(2) *Environmental factors*: punishment cannot be extended to any substantial degree beyond the individual offender, since no other person has the degree of guilt for the offence which would be acceptable as a prerequisite for punishment. But treatment can be applied beyond the individual who committed the act, to others, an alteration in whose behaviour might result in a substantial improvement in that individual.

(3) *The needs of the individual*: the "crime–responsibility–punishment" concept, because the punishment must fit the crime, may inhibit the court in ordering the treatment the offender needs. Indeed, it may work in the other direction, for example, in the case of the offender before the court for an offence which, in the eyes of the law, is comparatively minor, but which has

27

causes which require long-term treatment. The court cannot, in such circumstances, impose what would be considered a heavy punishment; indeed, the causes of the crime might well be regarded as mitigating circumstances which would make a lighter than normal punishment appropriate. No such difficulties would arise on the "preventive" principle since there the prime consideration would be the need for treatment measures.

(4) *Alteration of treatment*: somewhat similar considerations apply in relation to alteration of treatment. Punishment by its nature is "once for all". The criminal is entitled to ask that the judge should decide his punishment on the information available at the time of his conviction and, once the judge has weighed out the appropriate punishment, there are no good grounds for its alteration, since the acts which merited it have been done and cannot alter. Subsequent mitigation of punishment—shortening of treatment because of good response to treatment—may be acceptable, but the court, because its essential function is the taking of final decisions alterable only by a higher court, is not felt to be a suitable instrument for achieving this. This concept, however, is unhelpful from the point of view of treating or training an individual. Even were our knowledge about causes of crime and the reformation of offenders much fuller than it is, it is inconceivable that a court could ever guarantee to have chosen, at the moment of the commencement of its sentence, the exact treatment—to be given perhaps over a period of years—appropriate to the individual person before it. A doctor treating even a comparatively well-understood disease could not operate in this way. The doctor prescribes a course of treatment and observes the patient's response to it over a period. On the basis of his observations he continues the treatment or prescribes a different course, more drastic or less, as the situation appears to him to require. But he does not continue a course of treatment where, as a result of his observations, he is satisfied that it is doing no good, or that it has served its purpose and its continuation is either unnecessary or positively harmful.

THE CRIMINAL LAW AS APPLIED TO JUVENILES

55.   Turning to the criminal law as applied to juveniles, which is, of course the specific field within our remit, we find that while the general principles are inherently the same as we have described earlier, the balance has been modified in several important respects, the main modifications being that—

(1) The common law, while assuming the criminal responsibility of juveniles, accepts that youth may be a mitigating factor. This appears to be a recognition of the varying moral and intellectual capacity of children; and in some significant sense marks them off, for the purposes of the criminal law, from adults. If the fact of youth is in itself a mitigating factor, this seems to represent an important qualification of the "crime–responsibility–punishment" concept.

(2) Statute law imports the "welfare" of the child as a major consideration. While it is arguable that this concept is not completely unknown in the general criminal law, it is certainly not stated in explicit form. In relation to juveniles, it appears to have similarities to the civil law concept in relation to custody and guardianship, i.e., it presupposes in relation to the parents that in certain circumstances their wishes may be overridden and the child

removed from their control—society *pro tempore* assuming parental rights. To the child, the idea of penal measures being imposed for his welfare must often be hard, if not impossible, to understand; it presupposes the same concept—*in loco parentis*—the measures being imposed on the child as by a father on the basis, "It's for your own good". Thirdly, "welfare" looks not to the past act itself, but to the whole surrounding circumstances and above all to the future; and therefore implies a "preventive" or protective concept rather than judging the offence and the punishment which it deserves.

(3) The general criminal law is not greatly concerned with motive and cause. In relation to a juvenile, the natural question must be—why did he do it? Statute law provides for the furnishing of background reports in every case (other than trivial). This appears to be a fairly explicit application of the "preventive" concept.

56.   These three considerations together place heavy emphasis on the "preventive" concept; and the resultant conflict between the two principles to which we have already referred is in practice brought out even more sharply in the juvenile court than in the adult criminal court. For example—

(i) committal to an approved school is often seen by parents and child as a punishment out of all proportion to the gravity of the offence committed;

(ii) of two offenders dealt with for petty theft one is sent to an approved school; and the other to detention in a remand home. (The background reports show the first to be a persistent offender, over-indulged at home and in need of radical treatment. The second needs a short, sharp lesson.) The parents of the first regard the punishment as altogether out of proportion to the offence, and " unfair " as between the two offenders convicted of the joint offence;

(iii) a very high proportion of juvenile offenders are dealt with by admonition and by absolute discharge. On the basis of the offences committed this may be justified; a high proportion of those subsequently graduating to approved schools and borstal probably start off in this way. On the "preventive" principle, custodial or other more positive treatment at a much earlier stage might have more chance of success, but is ruled out as being altogether out of proportion to the gravity of the offence;

(iv) a child pleads guilty to theft of lead from derelict tenements. He undoubtedly realises that in some sense he did wrong. The parents' attitude is that the local authority should have had the buildings fenced off, if not under watch. Against such a parental outlook, where parental standards are in conflict with those of society, it is clearly difficult to regard the child as responsible for his actions.

57.   We do not believe that this apparent conflict of aim can ever be wholly eradicated, though the arrangements which we discuss later in our Report are capable, we believe, of reducing considerably such conflicts in the eyes of the parents, if less frequently in the eyes of the child. It would, however, be unrealistic to imagine that cases will not continue in which public measures for a child's protection and future welfare will still be seen as amounting to compulsion and punishment. Such attitudes, even if diminished, will remain as an inherent feature in the situation which has to be faced by those to whom the child's supervision and further training may be entrusted by public action. Attitudes of the kind are, of course, not confined to situations proceeding only

from court action in relation to juvenile offenders, but may be found—possibly even more strongly on occasion—in situations where a child is removed from the home as being in need of care or protection.

CARE OR PROTECTION PROCEEDINGS

58. It is useful to contrast at this point committal on grounds of need for care or protection. This is a civil, not a criminal, proceeding. At first sight, the distinction is a clear and simple one. The child has committed no criminal offence but on the basis of certain defined facts and circumstances is alleged to be in need of care or protection. Proceedings are taken by petition, not on criminal complaint, and from the outset the whole surrounding circumstances and background are in issue. The truth or otherwise of the allegation that the child is in need of care or protection is determined on the basis of the facts and general surrounding circumstances as presented, and is decided on standards of evidence provided for by the civil law, i.e., on standards of probability which are less stringent than those demanded in a criminal prosecution. "Care or protection" proceedings in fact represent an extension of the "preventive" principle, in that they may entail the application of compulsory measures in situations where no criminal offence may have been committed either by the child or the parent. Questions of criminal responsibility do not arise.

59. We have no reason to think that "care or protection" procedure does not meet with fairly general acceptance. As indicated in Chapter I, the procedure is comparatively rarely invoked. It may be that in present-day circumstances situations so deplorable as to justify proceedings for criminal neglect are less frequent than formerly.* It is, we think, also the case that, notwithstanding the difference in the standard of evidence in criminal and civil procedure, the criterion of need for care or protection as defined in the 1937 Act is such as to require evidence by the petitioner of weighty and fairly specific facts and circumstances justifying the need for intervention. By comparison, the presentation of evidence of an offence committed by a juvenile, related to a specific act on a specific occasion, may be a relatively simple matter. Nevertheless, we think it important to recognise that "care or protection" procedure is an implicit recognition of the "preventive" principle, which may be applied in circumstances in which no criminal offence has been committed by child or parent; in which the standards of evidence are in principle less stringent than those applied in criminal proceedings; but from which the consequences, in terms of interference between parent and child, may in practice be indistinguishable from those ensuing from a finding of guilt in relation to a juvenile offender. The tenor of much of the evidence we received was, as we have indicated, that these legal classifications, while relevant as pinpointing a series of definable facts or circumstances, were ultimately of significance only in so far as they indicated an underlying unsatisfactory situation calling for public intervention which might take any one of a wide variety of forms. Their true significance could be judged only on a thorough assessment of the surrounding facts and circumstances, and only on that basis could the child's

---

* The annual number of persons proceeded against for cruelty to children in each of the five-yearly periods ending in the years shown below was as follows:

1914	1930	1938	1962
682	209	319	295

needs be decided and his further training taken in hand with any realistic prospect of success. Under "care or protection" procedure (and this can be taken as including proceedings relating to persistent truants and children beyond parental control) that whole background is put clearly in issue as affording a reasonable, objective, factual basis on which to assess the child's needs, which are judged accordingly. The true needs of juvenile offenders on the other hand cannot always be so freely and objectively judged as a result of the nature of criminal procedure which, even with the modifications already introduced by statute, still imposes constraints on those to whom the task of adjudication is entrusted, in that the measures applied are in danger of being scaled down out of regard to the nature of the offence viewed in itself, and the scale of punishment appropriate thereto.

CONSIDERATIONS WHICH HAVE GOVERNED THE APPLICATION OF CRIMINAL PROCEDURE TO CHILDREN

60.   Such considerations inevitably raise questions as to the appropriateness of applying criminal procedure to juveniles. As already indicated, the criminal law assumes a high degree of personal responsibility and, though the law recognises youth as a mitigating factor which may be relevant to sentence or disposal, the concept of responsibility is still inherent and fundamental to the initial adjudication issue of guilt or innocence. It has, of course, always been recognised that the personal and moral responsibility of children may vary widely, age itself offering no reliable guide.

61.   Equally, a child's capacity to distinguish right and wrong, i.e., his intellectual knowledge of moral standards, may, though well developed even at an early age, not be accompanied by a corresponding degree of emotional maturity which would enable him to act on that knowledge. Again, for a child an active moral sense—as distinct from intellectual knowledge—is developed through practical insight, gained from those with whom he is in the closest day-to-day contact and relationships, these insights being acquired not through formal instruction but from practical experience and example of others in so far as they themselves give practical embodiment to certain standards. Difficult questions for the child may equally arise where the standards of the home and of his immediate associates are in conflict with those generally accepted by society; or for that matter where it appears to the child that there is a marked discrepancy between generally accepted standards, as conveyed to him at home and in school, and the actual practice of other individuals with whom he comes into contact in society.

62.   The legal presumption as to age of criminal responsibility, contained in section 55 of the Children and Young Persons (Scotland) Act, 1937, is one of the comparatively few conclusive presumptions of the law, and it shares with such presumptions this characteristic; it enshrines a proposition which is not necessarily true. It is because the proposition may or may not be true, and because it is considered expedient that the law should provide that matters are to be regulated on the basis of the universal truth of the proposition, that the questioning of the truth of the proposition is for practical purposes prohibited. We think it is important, in considering this aspect of the problems before us, to realise that the age of criminal responsibility has been laid down for purely legalistic reasons; it cannot possibly be said that the age so laid down either bears, or was ever intended to bear, any relation to the observable phenomena of child life.

63.   A glance at the common law of Scotland will show just what it was that influenced the selection of certain ages beyond which certain consequences in law were attracted. The common law is conveniently set out in Alison's Commentaries on the Criminal Law, published in 1832. The author divides those of less than full age into three categories:—

(1) "Minors, whether male or female, who have attained the age of 14 years are liable to any punishment, not excepting death itself for grave offences."

(2) "'Pupils', those below 14 years of age, may, though only 9, 10 or 11 years of age, be subject to an arbitrary punishment if they appear qualified to distinguish right from wrong, but not to the pain of death."

As instances, the author quotes two cases occurring in 1827, one of a boy aged 9 sentenced to 18 months hard labour, and another of two boys aged 13 who were sentenced to be transported for 14 years.

(3) "Children under 7 years of age are held to be incapable of crime and not the object of any punishment."

And in a further comment on this category he says, "At that tender age whatever vice exists must be ascribed to improper tuition or bad example, and the child cannot be considered as answerable for a violation of what he could not understand."

64.   There is one very striking feature of the doctrine of the common law of Scotland as laid down by Alison, a feature indeed which provides the justification for the existence of the doctrine at all. It will be noticed that each category is related to forms of punishment. Minors may be punished by death, pupils may not be punished by death but may be punished by any arbitrary punishment, and children under 7 years of age may not be punished at all. Looked at from this point of view the doctrine makes sense, otherwise it does not. It is quite understandable that the conscience of society should have revolted against the imposition of certain punishments upon children of less than a certain age. It is, however, quite outside human experience to assert that there is any age at which children change from being persons who are incapable of forming a criminal intention into persons who are capable of so doing. A moment's reflection will show that there was nothing about the climate of the year 1932 which could have justified anyone in Scotland saying, "At the age of 8 a child can be guilty of an offence whereas at the age of 7 he can not". Again, Alison justifies the rule that children under 7 are held incapable of crime by saying that the child cannot be considered as answerable for a violation of what he could not understand, and by, "answerable" the author means properly liable to be subjected to punishment. That may be true if the punishment of the law is being regarded, but it is certainly not true of other forms of punishment, which, being acts of regulatory discipline, are commonplace in every home from the age at which the objects of them may be held capable of reasoning at all. No witness who gave evidence before us was prepared to say that by clinical observation or otherwise it was possible to come to a conclusion that chronological age as such has any direct bearing on the capacity to form a criminal intent and to commit a crime.

65.   The legal presumption by which no child under the age of 8 can be subjected to criminal proceedings is not therefore a reflection of any observable fact, but simply an expression of public policy to the effect that in no circumstances should a child under the age of 8 be made the subject of criminal

proceedings and thus liable to the pains of the law. Equally, at various intermediate stages prior to adulthood, the effect of statute law is to exempt juveniles below certain ages from certain forms of judicial action. Thus, legislation restricts the imprisonment of offenders between the ages of 17 and 21, the committal to borstal training of juvenile offenders under the age of 16, and (save in exceptional circumstances) committal to an approved school of a child under the age of 10. It is clear, therefore, that the "age of criminal responsibility" is largely a meaningless term, and that in so far as the law refers to the age of 8 as being the minimum age for prosecution, this is essentially the expression of a practical working rule determining the cases in which a procedure which may result in punishment can be applied to juveniles.

CONSIDERATIONS APPLYING IN OTHER FIELDS OF LAW

66.   The legal presumption to which we have referred is a presumption for the purposes of criminal proceedings. Looking to various other fields, and in particular to more recent statute law, the position is at first sight somewhat confusing. As one witness put it graphically—

"8   —under this age a child is not criminally responsible.
10   —under this age a child must not—other than exceptionally—be sent to an approved school.
12   —the age at which a girl can acquire a separate domicile.
13   —under this age a child may not be employed.
14   —under this age is a child for the purposes of the 1937 Act.
14–21   —the age group for detention centre training.
15   —must attend school up to this age.
16–21   —the age group for borstal training.
16   —under this age may not marry.
16   —under this age may not purchase cigarettes.
17   —under this age is still subject to the juvenile court.
17   —under this age, and over 14 is a "young person".
17   —under this age cannot be sent to prison.
17   —under this age may not be employed in street trading.
18   —under this age may not purchase liquor."

The result of these restrictions as expressed shortly by this witness may be said to be as follows—

"At 12 a girl may leave home, but for the next year until 13 she may not be employed. She must attend school until she is 15. She may not purchase cigarettes until she is 16. She may marry at 16, but she is still subject to the jurisdiction of the juvenile court until she reaches the age of 17, and may not purchase a bottle of stout until she is 18, by which time she may be a wife and a mother."

67.   It seems clear from these examples that the various age limits in question cannot be justified on any narrow basis of fact. They are simply a broad recognition of the varying capacity and development of children at various ages. In the eyes of the civil law and the law relating to social and educational provision children are not regarded as completely free agents, and over a wide variety of fields of civil responsibility are debarred from rights of choice available to adults. Under the civil law a child in pupillarity is held to be in a state of absolute incapacity. He has no "person" in the legal sense of the word,

and is incapable of acting or even consenting. In civil law the state of pupillarity (i.e., under 14 in the case of boys and under 12 in the case of girls)—the period during which a child may be regarded as in a state of tutelage under his parents and undergoing education—has been accepted as disqualifying him entirely for those rights and responsibilities accruing to adult persons, and indeed this seems to us no more than a practical expression of what from the earliest times have been recognised to be the underlying facts of childhood. In contrast, it is only in the sphere of the criminal law that any different assumption operates. As we have seen, the legal presumption which the criminal law applies does not purport to reflect any objective facts about the actual age of attainment of responsibility, but was adopted as a practical rule with the object of exempting children of tender years from the pains of the law. Subsequent legislation has had the effect of modifying substantially the rigours of the law so far as disposal is concerned, and has introduced a further series of broad distinctions at later ages, the effect of which is to debar the application to children below those ages of various penalties and forms of custodial treatment. At the same time, the introduction of another form, of non-criminal proceeding, namely, "care or protection" proceedings—the practical effects of which may in many cases be indistinguishable from those taken against juvenile offenders—and indeed the emphasis which statute law places on the "welfare" of juvenile offenders, serve to indicate society's concern that effective preventive measures should be applied at the earliest possible stage wherever children come into trouble of such seriousness as to bring them within the ambit of the law. Since, however, judicial action in relation to juvenile offenders in all cases takes place within a framework governed by criminal procedure, the proceedings as a whole and in particular, the consideration of measures to be applied once the offence is established, cannot avoid being coloured by the underlying general concepts of responsibility and punishment which, for the reasons we have indicated in paragraph 54, may be positively detrimental in their practical application, in that they may inhibit the application of the preventive measures which the circumstances clearly demand, or the variation of measures already applied in circumstances in which it is clear that their continuance is serving no useful purpose. Moreover, as we have seen, the original reasons for exempting children of tender years from criminal proceedings—the rigours of the criminal law as operated in earlier times—have largely disappeared. It is, of course, arguable on the basis of observable fact that children under the age of 8 do sometimes commit acts amounting in law to criminal offences, and do so in the knowledge that they are doing wrong. There may well be occasions, e.g., where they are acting in concert with slightly older children, in which it would be equally appropriate even at that early age that they should be the subject of action under criminal, as distinct from "care or protection", procedure. Such cases would on any criterion be likely to be rare. What is undoubtedly of greater practical importance, however, is whether, in the light of the considerations already mentioned, the application of criminal procedure to juvenile delinquents above the age of 8 has compelling practical advantages, or whether delinquent children above that age might, in the interests of effective preventive measures, be better dealt with by some form of non-criminal procedure.

A SUGGESTED ALTERNATIVE

68. As we have indicated, "care or protection" proceedings offer an existing example of a procedure aimed at early preventive action and not involving criminal procedure. Some of our witnesses suggested—again on the basis of

some of the arguments discussed above—that all children below a certain age (for example, 10, 12 or 15), whether alleged as at present to be in need of "care or protection" or alleged offenders, should be brought before a juvenile court on petition. The basis of action in all cases would be the child's need for protection and training as shown by the facts alleged, irrespective of whether these facts consisted of a delinquent act or acts, or comprised other general facts and circumstances showing a clear need for protective and training measures. On that basis, children below the specified age-limit would be deemed to be incapable of committing crimes or offences, and delinquents below that age would then be brought before a juvenile court on the basis that they had committed acts which, if done by an adult, would amount to crimes or offences.

69. We see little advantage in a change of this kind, which to some extent seems to us little more than one of nomenclature. One consequence of such procedure would, however, be that, since the proceedings would be of a civil nature, all cases would be determined on civil law standards of probability, rather than on the criminal law standard under which the court has to be satisfied beyond reasonable doubt. In theory, this could result in the acquittal of a child or young person only slightly above the specified age-limit after trial for an offence, whereas a younger associate in the acts in question, brought before the court under "care or protection" procedure (in which the whole background circumstances would be in issue from the outset and in which proof would rest only on a balance of probabilities), would be the subject of judicial action. While the practical force of such objections has, we think, sometimes been overstated, this does not alter the question of principle. We consider that the present grounds which the law recognises as properly affording a basis for "care or protection" proceedings should continue, subject to certain subsidiary amendments which we discuss later. It seems to us, however, that any attempt to determine the truth of an allegation, where this is founded on the commission of an act constituting a legal offence, on the basis of the present "care or protection" procedure is both artificial and inherently undesirable.

70. At present, action in relation to juvenile offenders is entirely dependent on the initial establishment of the specified acts alleged which, if established, amount to the commission of an offence. If society is prepared on the proof of such acts by juveniles to authorise fairly sustained measures of education and training—in the interests of the child for the prevention of crime and for his own longer-term well-being—on the basis of thorough and searching enquiry into the whole surrounding circumstances including the child's home background, it is clearly of paramount importance that the initial basis for action should be established beyond doubt by stringent and testing procedures. This is precisely what criminal procedure aims to do. As a practical method of ascertaining and resolving disputed questions of fact, where the facts alleged amount if proved to the commission of a legal offence, it has stood the test of time and we do not believe that any erosion of it would meet with acceptance. It is clear to us, therefore, that under any arrangements that may be devised for the adjudication of juvenile offences, any dispute as to the allegation of fact must be determined on the present standards of evidence under criminal procedure by a court of law. That issue—resulting in a judicial finding of fact— is, however, an entirely separate one and calls for quite different skills and qualities from those to be applied in deciding on the action to be taken in relation to delinquent children once the fact is established.

71. In some countries, this dichotomy of function is recognised by completely separating the two in practice. The courts of law are concerned solely with the establishment of the truth or otherwise of the allegation issue, the treatment of juvenile offenders then being entrusted entirely to a separate and specialised agency, whose sole function is the consideration and application of training measures on referrals from the courts. That agency has the widest possible discretion, within the legal powers of disposal conferred on it, to select those training measures appropriate to the needs of the individual child and to vary these subsequently as circumstances require. The shortcomings which cause dissatisfaction within the present juvenile court system (and this is no reflection on those who serve in such courts) seem to us to arise essentially from the fact that they seek to combine the characteristics of a court of criminal law with those of a specialised agency for the treatment of juvenile offenders, proceeding on a preventive and educational principle. On that principle the offence, while the essential basis of judicial action, has significance only as a pointer to the need for intervention. Its true significance will not necessarily be found on the basis of any pre-conceived standard, i.e., by viewing the offence simply as an act in isolation and judging its potential seriousness simply by the ready-made standard offered by the range of sanctions which the law (and thus society at large) attaches to the particular class of offences which it exemplifies. In our view, criminal procedure does undoubtedly affect the whole atmosphere and manner of proceedings in juvenile courts; it also colours the entirely separate stage of the proceedings at which, the issue of fact having been resolved, the question of practical action in the form of training measures appropriate to the needs of the individual offender falls to be resolved. The underlying conflict between the two separate principles cannot fail in practice to create confusions and misconceptions which may be present, consciously or otherwise, in the minds of the bench; which cannot fail to be reflected in the general atmosphere of the court; and which are thus liable to be carried over to those appearing before such courts. With experienced persons on the bench these inherent defects may to some extent be diminished, more especially where the bench consists of a single, full-time, legally qualified judge, accustomed to facing such distinctions and conflicts daily in so far as they are potentially present in any criminal proceedings, whether involving an adult or a child. Equally, where juvenile courts comprise a lay bench, there are on occasion risks that out of a laudable desire to create an atmosphere conducive to the consideration of the child's treatment needs, the necessary degree of exactitude appropriate to the determination of the initial allegation issue, where disputed, may sometimes be overlooked, and unintentioned irregularities may develop.

A NEW ALTERNATIVE

72. Such considerations seem to us to point to the desirability of separating clearly the two issues of (*a*) adjudication of the allegation issue, and (*b*) consideration of the measures to be applied. However desirable such a change may appear to be in principle, it may be felt to raise practical problems, involving major changes of organisation and machinery, of such magnitude as to be unworkable in the conceivable future. We have therefore sought to examine how far in practice questions arising on the allegation issue occur, since clearly it is only in these cases that under the scheme discussed there is any disputed question at that stage falling to be resolved by criminal process before a court of law.

73. The consensus of opinion among our witnesses, supported by inquiries which we addressed to a representative cross-section of juvenile courts in Scotland (which together dealt with about two-thirds of all juveniles proceeded against), indicated that in almost 95 per cent of the cases there is no dispute as to the facts alleged, those concerned pleading guilty. In such a situation no evidence is led, the allegation issue thus being determined not by the court but by the admission of the accused. Only the remainder—around 5 per cent—pled not guilty and thus proceeded to trial. In the light of these facts, it seems to us entirely practicable to devise a procedure whereby juvenile offenders would in all cases be brought before a specialised agency whose sole concern would be the measures to be applied on what amounts to an agreed referral. Under such a procedure on appearance, the child and his parents would be asked whether they fully understood the nature of the allegation and in the parents' presence the child would then be asked whether or not he admitted to having done the acts alleged. If this was admitted, the agency would then proceed to deal with the child. If the child denied the act in question, action by the agency would be stayed, and the case would immediately be referred to the Sheriff Court, which would thereupon have jurisdiction to determine under criminal procedure the disputed allegation of fact. Where the Court found the facts established, the case would thereupon revert to the agency, which would then be empowered to consider measures of treatment in the same way as on an "agreed" case. The agency would thus exercise jurisdiction only on the basis of facts established by admission of the child in the parents' presence and with their agreement, or after an adjudication by a court of law. It would have no concern whatsoever with the determination of legal issues, its sole function being the consideration and application of training measures appropriate to the child's needs. Such an agency would clearly not be a criminal court of law, or indeed a court in any accepted sense. It would be the duly constituted public agency authorised to deal with juvenile offenders, where necessary by the application of compulsory measures. Within the range of measures authorised by law, it would have the widest discretion in their application appropriate to the needs of the individual child, who would thereafter remain within its jurisdiction for as long a period as was judged to be necessary, subject to whatever upper-age limit might be fixed by statute. During that period the agency would have the widest discretion to vary or terminate the measures initially applied, and where appropriate to substitute others.

74. For convenience of discussion at this stage, we shall refer to this agency as the "panel", as distinct from the courts of law. The panel would consist on any given occasion of three persons drawn from a list for the area in question—all of whom would be selected at the outset as being persons who either by knowledge or experience were considered to be specially qualified to consider children's problems. They would be essentially a lay body, and while in practice their numbers might well include members of the legal profession, doctors, teachers, and local authority members, none would be appointed by reason of any existing official position or specialist qualification, but simply on the basis of personal qualities. It seems to us important that as a public authority vested with powers of compulsory action the panel should be seen to be an entirely independent agency, and the machinery of appointment should reflect that fact.

75. The panel would thus be neither a local authority committee nor a court of law. It would, however, by law be the duly constituted public authority

37

appointed to deal with juvenile offenders. Since the panel would be vested with coercive powers, e.g., in certain cases to order a child's removal from home, its decisions would be subject to a right of appeal to the Sheriff. We examine the powers and procedure in a later Chapter. The salient features to which we wish to draw attention at this stage are that—

(*a*) there is no question under such proposals of taking juvenile offenders outwith the ambit of the law. Under the proposals, a few exceptions apart, juvenile offenders would be dealt with not by criminal procedure, but by a special agency on whom this specialised jurisdiction would be conferred by law;

(*b*) such a panel would not be empowered to resolve disputed questions of fact, these being reserved to a court of law (the Sheriff Court);

(*c*) while the actual range of powers conferred on the panel would not in our view differ appreciably from those available to the present juvenile courts, the manner in which they could competently be exercised would be very different. In principle, a child would remain within the panel's jurisdiction up to whatever age-limit was fixed by statute, and during that period the measures applied could be terminated or varied (by substituting any of the methods of disposal within the panel's powers for that initially ordered). Since such arrangements clearly imply the possibility of more intensive and sustained measures of supervision and training than at present, including in some cases the child's removal from home for varying and initially indeterminate periods of residential training, it is clearly important that such decisions, involving as they do the possibility of major interventions between parent and child, should be open to judicial scrutiny on an appeal to the Sheriff.

76.   We do not wish to suggest that in the majority of cases such sustained measures would in fact be likely to be applied. In the majority of cases, we believe that the parents, whatever their shortcomings in the eyes of outsiders, are genuinely anxious for their children's well-being, and in many cases where consideration before the panel proceeded upon a basis of agreed facts the panel's decisions would be arrived at after extensive consideration and discussion with the parents, as a result of which it would be apparent to all concerned that the measures applied were determined on the criterion of the child's actual needs. In some cases, action would be agreed with the parents and would then proceed on an informal basis, i.e., without a formal order by the panel. In others, where a formal order was made placing the child under supervision, this would not necessarily be seen by the parents as unwarranted interference. Nevertheless, if these arrangements are to be in any way effective, we consider that they may be expected to result in a wider use of continuing supervision of the delinquent child within the community, and in some cases in a greater readiness to apply residential training measures involving removal from home at much earlier stages than apply at present. In so far as these arrangements imply sustained action from the earliest possible stage in the interests of prevention of more serious delinquency, we do not seek to deny that this would involve greater inroads into the home and family life by supervising officers nominated by the panel—all of which may be represented as unwarranted interference in the liberty of the individual. We have indicated, and discuss in more detail in a later Chapter, the rights of appeal which would be available against decisions by the panel—rights which in our view offer safeguards as great as are afforded under existing law, and which may well in practice be more effective.

77. A study of human history would no doubt show that in every age succeeding generations have in turn deplored the ways of youth. Alison's Commentaries, written in 1832, to which we have already referred, noted "the vast increase in juvenile delinquency". In our own century it was in earlier years fashionable to attribute delinquency in large measure to social and environmental factors. It had for long been observed that many of those convicted of delinquency came mainly from poorer elements largely to be found in certain districts of urban communities—districts whose names in time became, sometimes undeservedly, local or even national by-words. Improvement in economic and living standards and the development of the social services has not brought the improvement which on this view was to be looked for. It is, of course, the case that, while major advances in these directions have been achieved, there still remain substantial sectors within our society which that progress has only begun to touch. The environmental argument, it is now recognized, could, however, never offer a universal answer; in a great many delinquents a degree of maladjustment, of malfunction personal to the individual, has always been observable; and even in the so-called "delinquent" areas, the majority of the children do not come before the courts. Few parents actively teach their children to steal, although rather more may imply an unconventional system of values at odds with that of society at large. What does seem clear is that despite the social advances made, juvenile delinquency, while still affecting a small minority of the child population, has not diminished. It has kept pace with the increase in child population, and the increase has latterly shown some signs of outstripping a purely proportional growth. In consequence, there is, we believe, currently a fairly general, though not always clearly articulated, dissatisfaction with the apparent operation of the existing arrangements for dealing with juvenile offenders. As we have already indicated, we do not consider that this is a reflection on the existing juvenile courts, given the general framework and principles within which they are required to work. The problems daily confronting those courts go to the roots of human behaviour, and, however valuable the insights already or likely to be gained from research-based general studies, these problems cannot be resolved in terms appropriate to those of an exact science.

78. Ultimately the question must be resolved on practical grounds. Delinquency is predominantly an activity of the young. On purely practical grounds it would therefore appear that emphasis ought to be given to preventive and remedial measures at the earliest possible stage if more serious delinquencies are not to develop. That implies above all the application of an educative principle, which cannot hope to operate with any measure of success except under a procedure which from the outset seeks to establish the individual child's needs in the light of the fullest possible information as to his circumstances, personal and environmental. The establishment of those needs is in itself a task calling for essentially personal qualities of insight and understanding, which obviously cannot be guaranteed under any system of selection. None of the existing systems of selection can be said to start from such a basis, and, difficult and demanding though the duties are, we are confident that the alternative would be able to draw on a much wider field of suitable persons than is at present the case. The task of the new body calls for skills quite different from those involved in adjudicating legal issues, and it is quite inappropriate that it should be expected to combine the two functions.

79.   Further, since there is no "master-key to fit all cases", the criterion being that of the child's needs, it follows that the new body must be accorded, subject only to certain general limits laid down by law, an unfettered discretion not only initially to apply, but to modify or vary, the measures appropriate to the individual child.

80.   It must finally be a matter of judgement how far, in relation to juveniles and their parents, the application of an educative principle in this way would in fact and in practice represent an appreciable inroad into personal and family life, amounting to loss of liberty or freedom from interference such as to be unacceptable in our society. If, on such grounds, it were to be felt that a fuller recognition of the educative principle could not be accepted, it is necessary to face the practical alternatives. A return to a purer form of the "crime–punishment" concept seems altogether unacceptable. If that be so, society must consider whether it is satisfied with the *status quo* and is prepared to accept the social consequences. For our part we do not believe that a retention of the present system, resting as it does on an attempt to retain the two existing concepts in harness, is susceptible of modification in any way which would seem likely to make any real impact on the problem.

81.   Finally, if society's present concern is to find practical expression in a more discriminating machinery for intervention, it must be recognized that society's own responsibility towards the children concerned will be correspondingly increased, and that this will make commensurate demands on the nation's resources.

Part Two

CHAPTER IV

A New Machinery—The Juvenile Panels

82.   In the latter part of the preceding Chapter we have indicated in broad outline the considerations governing the constitution and operation of the juvenile panels which we envisage as replacing the existing juvenile courts. We now indicate in more detail the practical implications of our recommendation.

THE GUIDING FACTORS

83.   All three matters—constitution, powers and procedure—are closely interrelated. While examination of the powers of juvenile courts is often taken as meaning a consideration of the entire range of measures at their disposal, it is, we think, helpful at the present stage to note that the powers of the present juvenile courts are limited to powers of decision. They are in no sense executive agencies, and their powers, so far as treatment measures are concerned, are thus limited to deciding the particular treatment measures to be applied, their decisions being essentially in the form of orders or authorisations instructing various executive agencies, recognised as being specially qualified to do so, to carry out one or other of the treatment measures authorised by statute. Such measures having been instituted, the court's function is at an end. At present, the courts powers in this sense are limited to two broad classes of decisions— decisions authorising the child's supervision by various executive agencies within the community, and decisions committing the child to various forms of residential training (in many cases implying *de facto* the temporary assumption of parental rights by those responsible for the management of the homes or schools concerned).

84.   The following powers of the juvenile courts may be applied in relation to any of the classes of children brought before them, i.e., whether as juvenile offenders or as being in need of "care or protection":—

(1)   supervision (in the case of juvenile offenders under a probation order; in other cases, under a supervision order in which either a probation officer or some other supervising officer may be nominated);

(2) a requirement on the parents to find security for the child's care and guardianship or good behaviour;

(3)   committal to the care of a "fit person" (including the local authority);

(4)   committal to an approved school.

In relation to juvenile offenders, the courts have (or will have once the Criminal Justice (Scotland) Act, 1963, is fully in force) the following further powers:

(1)   deferred sentence;

(2)   admonition;

(3)   absolute discharge;

(4)   fine;

(5)   according to age—committal to a remand home (under an order for punitive detention), detention centre, borstal institution or young offenders institution.

85.   Over a comparatively wide field, the same range of measures is thus already regarded as being properly applicable to any child irrespective of the precise circumstances, in terms of legal category, in which he is brought before the courts. It is generally recognised that a fair proportion of juvenile offences, particularly among younger children, amount to acts of petty mischief which must be dealt with, but which are unlikely to call for elaborate and lengthy measures of training and supervision. It would, moreover, in the great majority of such cases be quite absurd to postulate either serious emotional disturbance in the child or parental neglect (unless that term is defined so widely as to go far beyond any currently accepted usage). On the other hand, there are undoubtedly cases in which either or both factors may be present, whether the grounds of action are at present juvenile offences or circumstances justifying care or protection proceedings. Over the whole field, equally there are numerous instances in which the children, and sometimes other members of the family as well, have already come to the notice in one way or another of various public agencies as being in trouble or difficulty, and in need of help and guidance: in such situations it may well be largely accidental that in individual cases the call for further measures is a consequence of the commission of an offence by the child.

86.   In recent years, there has been increasing public recognition of the need for early forestalling action in the case of children in need—such action being taken through a wide variety of public and voluntary agencies. It has been accepted that such needs cannot be met by treating the child in isolation but rather as a member of a family unit in a particular environment. The removal of factors adverse to the child has thus increasingly been seen to lie in the application of what is essentially an educational process—educational both for the child and his parents. What is implied is the continuing application, by persuasive action, of skilled advice and guidance, with the aim of evoking in turn from the parties concerned a constructive response, based on an increased awareness and understanding of their underlying problems and responsibilities. Such a process amounts essentially to one of helping others to help themselves. It cannot work without adequate machinery for early identification and diagnosis. The wide variety of public and voluntary agencies contributing to this field make it essential that there should be clear channels of communication for reporting all cases; and given the widely varying nature of family problems which diagnosis may bring to light, and the importance of bringing to bear the skills of the particular social worker or group of workers best fitted to meet those needs in any given case, co-ordination of effort is equally important at all subsequent stages. These principles have already received substantial recognition in relation to children in need (other than those coming before the juvenile courts) in the Children and Young Persons Act, 1963, which places new responsibilities on local authorities in these directions.

87.   It is, we think, accepted that more often than not the problem of the child who is in need and the delinquent child can be traced to short-comings in the normal "bringing-up" process—in the home, in the family environment and in the schools. What has, we think, not hitherto been equally recognised is that the question which confronts society (in the shape of the juvenile courts) in every

case is the essentially practical one, namely, the child's need for special measures, since the normal educational process has for whatever reason fallen short or failed to have effect. Our proposals ultimately imply no more than a full and realistic acceptance of that fact and the consequences flowing from it.

88.   The application of what is essentially an educational process in this way demands both a flexibility of approach and a continuing oversight and scrutiny of the actual measures being applied. These factors are, for reasons which we have discussed in the previous Chapter, present only to a limited extent under the present juvenile court arrangements. Under existing arrangements the individual measures to be applied are subject to various statutory time-limits. With certain exceptions, notably breach of probation and discharge of "fit person" orders and their replacement by other measures (e.g., of residential training), there is no general provision whereby an order, once made, may be reviewed, even where it may be clear at an early stage to the supervising agency concerned that the measures adopted are not achieving the result hoped for. Further formal action can in these circumstances only be taken in the event of even more serious circumstances arising, which justify the bringing of entirely fresh proceedings in consequence either of a further offence or of a situation justifying "care or protection" proceedings. Existing procedure, focused as it is on certain defined acts and situations, and resulting in training measures subject in most cases to preconceived, and in that sense arbitrary, limitations of time, is inimical to any idea of continuing educational process. Further, the agency (at present the juvenile court) responsible for deciding those measures, having made its determination, retains no continuing responsibility over the children concerned. The court's task is to determine what it considers to be the appropriate measures and to authorise their execution by one or other of a variety of social agencies, whether in the public or voluntary field. Equally, no formal means exist, nor is there any formal responsibility on anyone, to inform the juvenile courts in any particular case of the apparent effectiveness or otherwise of the measures applied. Moreover, while the range of social agencies responsible either for reporting initially or for executing the courts' decisions is fairly large, few of them can be said to be in really close day-to-day contact with the courts, whose decisions are thus necessarily limited to authorising executive action at the hand of agencies with whom they have little or no effective subsequent contact.

89.   The probation service apart, the existing social services concerned with children have developed independently of the juvenile courts. Under present arrangements, there is at the outset a duality of reporting agencies in that while the submission to the courts of social background reports is required by statute in all cases (other than trivial), those involving juvenile offenders are made by the probation service, and those involving juveniles in need of "care or protection" by the children's service. Moreover, while juvenile offenders are brought before the courts at the instance of the appropriate public prosecutor, a number of agencies (including the local authority, the police and the Royal Scottish Society for the Prevention of Cruelty to Children) are authorised to bring "care or protection" proceedings. Thus, while any one of the agencies mentioned may have been involved up to the point of the initial referral and in some cases also responsible for the social background reports, the degree to which they may be called upon to maintain continuing contact with the individual child will vary widely according to the disposal decided upon by the court. The court may entrust the child's further training to any of a variety of

agencies which at that stage may involve (if supervision within the community is decided on) either the probation or the children's department; or, if custodial measures result, the staff of institutions responsible to a variety of agencies (including children's committees, education authorities, approved school managers or other voluntary managers, or the Secretary of State, who is responsible for detention centres and borstals). Once such action has been taken, the court's effective responsibility ceases.

90.   Under the arrangements we propose, the juvenile panels will have a continuing jurisdiction over all children brought before them, subject only to a statutory upper age-limit. Below that age the panels will have complete discretion to alter or vary measures initially applied. These special educational measures would include both supervision within the community or, where appropriate, more intensive and usually shorter term periods of residential in-training, the completion of which would as part of a natural process normally be followed by resumed supervision on the child's return into the community. At all stages the child would remain within the panel's jurisdiction.

91.   It is essential to such arrangements that the panels should be provided with a single executive agency, comprising a chief officer (whom for brevity we shall call, at this stage, "the Director") and a suitably qualified staff of various disciplines (including qualified social workers) operating under his general direction. The Director would be responsible not only for the submission to the panel of social background reports in all cases (whatever the initial sources of referral), but for making recommendations to the panel as to the measures to be applied, and for exercising continuous oversight of all children who are subject to the panel's order. Apart from any specific direction for review of cases made by the panel itself, he would have complete discretion to report back to the panel at any time, where it appeared to him that the measures already ordered were not working well; and to make further recommendations accordingly. By that means, the panel through the Director would have continuing access to and oversight of the full range of measures at its disposal. In each case, the initial decision would be that special educational measures were required (thereby implying that the child would automatically become subject to the oversight of the Director as the panel's executive agent). This decision would in certain cases be amplified by the further order that the child should undergo additional special measures, e.g., a period of residential home or residential school training. In such situations, however, the child would remain within the panel's jurisdiction, and ultimate responsibility would not pass as at present to the managers of the home or school—continuous contact with the child being maintained through the Director. The organisation to provide these services—which we shall refer to as "the social education department"—its staffing, and the measure of reorganisation necessary for its creation—we discuss in a later Chapter*. Our proposals have to be seen as a comprehensive scheme, and we wish to make plain that we regard the provision of the new department (and the reorganisation which it implies) as essential to the operation of the juvenile panels which we are recommending. Unless the panels are provided with an executive agency—responsible for reporting, for recommending, and for supervision in all cases, we do not see how they can effectively discharge their responsibility for

---

* In view of references to education authorities in intermediate Chapters, we should make it clear at this stage that we do not think that the social education department should be divorced from the general education services. Like them, the authority responsible for providing the social education department should be the education authority.

continuing oversight on an adequately informed basis. Equally, unless such arrangements are accepted, implying the possibility of sustained and continuing educational measures beyond those which can be applied at present, we see little prospect of a truly effective treatment of juvenile offenders, which is the legitimate public aim. Against that background, we now discuss in more detail the arrangements for the constitution, powers and procedure of the juvenile panels.

CHAPTER V

The Constitution and Procedure of the Juvenile Panels

CONSTITUTION

92.   Broadly, and subject only to certain limited exceptions which we discuss in paragraphs 124–126, we recommend that those classes of children who are at present subject to the jurisdiction of the juvenile courts should in future be dealt with by the juvenile panels. Each panel should at any given sitting comprise three persons. Panels should be set up in each education authority area, their number and location being determined in each case by the appropriate Sheriff. For this purpose it would be the Sheriff's duty from time to time to appoint a sufficient number of persons to serve on the panels, and to designate a chairman and two deputy chairmen for each. In making appointments the Sheriff should have the widest discretion, subject only to the general considerations that—

(*a*)   those selected should be in his opinion persons who are specially qualified either by knowledge or experience to consider children's problems.

(*b*)   appointments should be such as to ensure wherever practicable the presence of a woman member at any sitting of an individual panel.

(*c*)   while the list of persons appointed should be sufficiently numerous to staff the membership of the panels, bearing in mind that in almost all cases service will be in a voluntary and part-time capacity, acceptance of appointment would be expected to imply willingness to serve on the panel regularly and for a continuous period of not less than three months annually.

(*d*)   the appropriate education authority, in its capacity as the authority responsible for providing the "social education department" which we are recommending, should be required at such intervals as may be provided to submit for this purpose a list of persons (who may or may not be local authority members) to the Sheriff.

93.   The last recommendation has to be read in the light of our detailed proposals, discussed in a later Chapter, for reorganisation of existing local social services concerned with the needs of children. For the reasons there indicated, we are recommending the unification of those services in a new department under the education authority, and it seems to us appropriate that to this extent the local authority having statutory responsibilities in this sphere should be associated in the constitution of the panels, in a manner which will at the same time maintain the principle of independent appointment at the hand of the Sheriff.

94.　Appointments would be for a period of three years, and members would be eligible for re-appointment, subject to an age-limit of 65 (at which all appointments would in any event terminate).

95.　Such arrangements bear certain similarities to those governing the appointment of the juvenile courts in the four areas in relation to which Orders have been made under Section 50 of the Children and Young Persons (Scotland) Act, 1937. In these areas, however, the membership of the juvenile courts is drawn from the body of justices as a whole. Our proposals on the other hand are in no way linked with the appointment of justices and pre-suppose a system of direct appointment by the Sheriff.

MACHINERY FOR REFERRAL TO THE PANEL

96.　At present the decision whether or not to institute criminal proceedings in any particular case rests with the appropriate public prosecutor, who is entirely independent of the police. This principle applies equally to juvenile offenders. Juveniles alleged to be in need of "care or protection" are dealt with under non-criminal procedure, and may under statutory provisions be brought before a juvenile court by the police, the local authority and other "authorised persons", e.g., the R.S.S.P.C.C. In certain areas, we understand that the actual presentation before the court of the petition alleging need for "care or protection" is handled on behalf of the local authority by the public prosecutor (where there is a full-time prosecutor) or, in cases where the petition relates to further proceedings with a view to committal of a child already in local authority care under the Children Act, 1948, by the probation service. In both of these situations it has, we understand, been felt to be advantageous that the court should have the assistance of an independent official who is not strictly a party to the case and can be relied upon to present an impartial viewpoint.

97.　The issues before the proposed juvenile panels will in future—as we have indicated—be entirely confined to decisions about treatment measures, and will not be concerned with disputed questions of fact. It might thus be thought that the presentation of cases before the panels could well be handled throughout by the director of the appropriate social education department. We are, however, proposing that any dispute about the factual basis of the allegation should be decided by a court of law (the Sheriff Court), and whether or not the allegation is disputed will be known only on the child's first appearance before the juvenile panel. It is accordingly important that any case before presentation should continue to be the subject of scrutiny by an independent official possessing the necessary qualifications to enable him to determine whether there is *prima facie* sufficient evidence in law to support a referral to the panel. This is in fact essentially the first question which the public prosecutor has to consider in every prosecution at present. The prosecutor has, however, the further duty of deciding whether, assuming that in his view there is such evidence, the nature of the offence is in itself of such public importance as to justify a prosecution. At present, therefore, in a number of cases involving juveniles, prosecutors may decide simply to take no proceedings or to deal with the matter by warning, almost invariably in the case of juveniles, administered on their instructions by the police. Under our proposals, since the test will be whether special educational measures are required, the nature of this latter discretion will be substantially changed; and the advice of the director will clearly be an important consideration. But the question may obviously in certain cases involve a difficult and delicate exercise of discretion in assessing where the public interest truly lies, and so far as our proposals are concerned, we do not consider that the decision whether or not a referral should be made to the juvenile panel can be left to the initial reporting agencies (whether the police or the local social services).

THE "REPORTER" TO THE PANEL

98.   We therefore recommend that referral to the juvenile panels should in each area be at the instance of a single independent official, who to that extent would be exercising functions having similarities to those of a public prosecutor. In practice, however, the actual handling of cases, as they proceed before the juvenile panels, will rarely raise legal issues, and will for the most part be concerned with the measures to be applied in the child's best interests. On that basis the presentation of cases before the panels seems to us to call for a degree of practical knowledge and understanding of children's problems which cannot readily be combined as at present with the role of public prosecutor, whose functions are necessarily concerned primarily with questions of prosecution arising from adult crime. Since therefore it seems to us that the referral of cases to the juvenile panels should be in the hands of an independent official competent to assess both the legal issues (in so far as these are involved) and also the wider question of the public interest, he should preferably be an officer combining a legal qualification with a period of administrative experience relating to the child welfare and educational services. Working in close touch with such services, this officer would be independent of any of them. The decision whether or not to make a referral to the panel would rest entirely with him. All reports, whether from the police or other statutory or voluntary agencies, would be made to his office without distinction as to whether the basis of referral were founded on delinquent acts or on facts or circumstances such as might at present be thought to justify "care or protection" proceedings. In situations of the latter kind, the present powers of various public agencies and "authorised persons" to institute referrals at their own hand would thus be abolished.

99.   Prosecutions in Scotland are, as already indicated, almost invariably and with few exceptions brought by the appropriate public prosecutor. This practice applies equally to juvenile offenders. Prosecution of juveniles at the instance of private persons is for practical purposes unknown. Certain public bodies are, however, excepted from the general rule, the major exception being prosecutions at the instance of the British Transport Commission, who, on reports by the British Transport Police, are authorised to bring before a juvenile court juvenile offenders involved in offences (in practice, malicious damage and theft) involving railway property. We understand that in 1961 such prosecutions involved 1,019 children and young persons. The prosecutions were in all cases brought before Sheriff Courts, except in the four areas in which specially constituted J.P. Juvenile Courts at present operate. We can see no justification for the continuance of this procedure under our proposals. Indeed, it seems to us important that the same criteria should from the outset be applied in all cases, and on similar grounds we have already recommended the abolition of the power of "authorised persons" to bring "care or protection" proceedings. On the same basis, "railway" offences involving juveniles would, under our proposals, be

reported by the British Transport Police to the appropriate reporter responsible for referrals, who would as in any other case decide whether or not the case should be brought before the panel. We recommend accordingly.

100.   As well as deciding on individual referrals to the panel, this official, whom we describe as "the reporter", would act as legal adviser to the panel as necessary. He would also be responsible, in the event of referrals about disputed issues of fact, or appeals against decisions of the panels, for presentation of the evidence or, as the case may be, the reasons underlying the panel's decision, before the Sheriff Court. He would also be responsible for maintaining formal records of the panel's decisions and for their formal intimation to those entrusted with the child's care. In so far as the panel might instruct review of cases already under their jurisdiction, it would be his duty to see that further reports were timeously made.

101.   The reporter would, of course, require to be provided with accommodation and clerical assistance. With such arrangements we see no need for a separate appointment of clerk to the panel. In so far as the panel may to a limited extent need legal advice, this would be provided by the reporter. In practice we envisage that a member of his staff would attend in order to record the panel's proceedings, the actual presentation of the cases to be considered being made by the reporter himself.

102.   Given the combination of qualities to be looked for, we do not consider it possible to lay down hard and fast qualifications for the office. We do, however, for the reasons already indicated, attach importance to a legal qualification, though this alone is in our view far from being the sole qualification. The range of experience to be looked for might well be found among officers employed in County or Town Clerks' departments, who have acted as clerks to children's committees or probation committees. We appreciate, however, that this can be no more than an illustration of the type of qualification and experience to be looked for. At the same time, the duties of reporter to the panel and the responsibilities entailed are such as to make these appointments fundamental to the operation of the scheme as a whole. In view of the independent nature of his office, it seems to us appropriate that such appointments should be made by the Sheriff, the costs, together with that of the panels as a whole, being met by the appropriate local education authority. In his particular field, the reporter should enjoy a special independent status, and the exercise of his day-to-day functions should not be the subject of education authority scrutiny. In the matter both of appointment and removal from office, the decision should rest with the Sheriff.

THE PANEL'S EXECUTIVE ARM

103.   The duties of the reporter to the panel, as we have described them, involve—

    (a)   all decisions as to initial referrals,

    (b)   the handling of appeals against the panel's decisions,

    (c)   administrative responsibility for the general ordering of the panel's business.

104.   These duties are clearly different from those involved either in the provision of social background reports, of making initial or subsequent recommendations about treatment, or of maintaining continuous oversight of children subject to the panel's directions. The latter functions, which are

essentially of an executive nature, call for a high degree of specialist skill, training and experience in social work. The chief executive officer (the "Director") of the department to carry out these functions would, as we have indicated, be responsible to the panel for (a) social background reports in all cases referred to the panel and (b) for making recommendations (initial or subsequent) for treatment measures in any individual case. On the panel's deciding to apply special educational measures, he would be responsible in every case for seeing that they were carried out either by the staff of his own department or some other local service or, in cases in which residential training was involved in establishments not directly under his control, for exercising continuing oversight of the child's progress and for reporting further to the panel at any time, either on their instruction or on his own initiative. His department would in each area be the central co-ordinating channel of information to the panel on all matters bearing on the child's treatment needs. He would in all matters affecting initial referrals to the panel act in close consultation with the reporter to the panel. Initial referrals would, however, as previously indicated, be at the instance of the reporter, who as an independent official would be the final arbiter of such referrals. In all matters relating to the treatment needs of children referred to them, however, the director of the social education department would be the panel's recognised source of informed advice, and he would at any subsequent time be free to make recommendations to them, in the light of the child's progress, for the alteration or variation of the measures initially decided upon. He would thus in all treatment matters be the panel's executive agent, directly responsible to them for all children under their jurisdiction.

PROCEDURE BEFORE THE JUVENILE PANELS

105. As we have indicated, all referrals to the panel should be at the instance of the reporter. The form of referral should in each case consist of a short statement of the facts and circumstances constituting the grounds of the referral.

106. Where a police report is made to the reporter, a copy should simultaneously be sent to the director of the social education department. This procedure would replace the provisions under Section 43 of the Children and Young Persons (Scotland) Act, 1937, for notice to be given to the probation or children's departments. Where a case is referred to the reporter by any other person, the reporter should similarly arrange for the preparation of a social background report by the director of the social education department.

107. The reporter would also be required to send notice to both parents, setting out shortly the basis of the referral and the place and time at which they were expected to attend. While we recognise that it is very desirable that both parents should attend before the panels, we appreciate that it would be impracticable to insist on this in every case. In many cases at present, only the child's mother attends, the father being at work. We consider that the normal practice should be to notify both parents, and that in every case the panel should inquire as to the reasons for failure of one of the parents to attend, and should in any appropriate case if necessary consider an adjournment to enable his or her attendance.

108. On appearance before the panel, the first step would be to explain the grounds of the referral to the child and his parents. Where considered appropriate, the child could be seen separately from the parents, and the parents

from the child. Thereafter, if the grounds of referral are disputed, proceedings would be stayed, and the case referred by the reporter on a petition to the Sheriff.

109.   Within that general framework and bearing in mind that discussions in the panel will in almost all cases be directed solely to the treatment measures which can most appropriately be applied, we do not consider that it is either necessary or desirable to seek to lay down any rigid framework governing the panel's proceedings. The questions arising are in our view likely to emerge most clearly only in an atmosphere of full, free and unhurried discussion, as a result of which the underlying aim and intention is made apparent to all concerned. We would expect that in many cases it would be possible to enlist the co-operation of the parents from the outset, and as a result adopt appropriate measures informally and by agreement without resort to an order by the panel. Some of the witnesses who appeared before us, who were in general sympathy with this aim, described the intention as being to create something of a "committee" atmosphere. We doubt whether such a description is altogether appropriate. If the desired atmosphere is to be achieved, the proceedings must in our view be conducted in all cases in private, and only the parties and officials directly concerned should be present. Indeed, bearing in mind that the proceedings will in every case entail the presence of three panel members, the reporter and a clerical assistant, as well as the child and his parents, we think it important that the number of social workers and other specialist advisers whose attendance may be required should at any given point be kept to a minimum, so that the sittings of the panel should not be such as to convey the impression of a large gathering of people. Responsibility for the ordering of the panel's business will in this respect lie with the reporter, and it will be for him to ensure, in conjunction with the director of social education (he himself or one of his staff of course being present), that, where information supplementary to the initial social background report is required, this is so far as possible made available by means of further written reports from the specialist advisers concerned.

REFERRALS AND APPEALS TO THE SHERIFF

110.   We have already recommended that, in event of any dispute as to the grounds on which a referral to the panel is made, the proceedings should be stayed and the case referred on a petition to the Sheriff. The Sheriff should then be empowered to make an order authorising the panel to exercise jurisdiction, if satisfied that the grounds of the referral have been made out. In hearing such an application, the procedure before the Sheriff would follow as nearly as may be that in the case of a complaint by the procurator fiscal, or of a "care or protection" petition, where the facts are disputed. In the hearing of such referrals, the Sheriff's function would be the normal function of a court of law in determining disputed issues of fact on the standards of evidence laid down by law. He would either sustain or dismiss the referral.

111.   Appeals to the Sheriff raise somewhat different issues. While we contemplate that in an appreciable number of cases the juvenile panels will be able to proceed with the agreement of the parents, there will undoubtedly remain a number in which compulsory orders will have to be made, including those involving the child's removal from home and from parental control. Such disputes will not, of course, involve any legal issue of fact, the question simply

being whether the measures ordered are in all the circumstances warranted in the interests of the child, or whether they amount to unjustified interference between parent and child amounting to unwarranted infringement of individual liberty. Such issues, which essentially represent a dispute between the parents and the duly constituted public authority authorised to deal with such questions, can, we believe, be resolved in a manner acceptable to public opinion only on an appeal to a judicial officer, in this case the Sheriff. Such appeals are likely to arise most frequently on decisions involving custodial treatment, and the panel's order should in all such cases record briefly the reasons for its decision. The right of appeal should, however, apply in relation to all orders made by the juvenile panel, written intimation of appeal to be lodged with the reporter within seven days of the making of the order. The appeal should thereupon be intimated immediately to the Sheriff Clerk by the reporter, and the appeal should be heard within seven days thereafter.

112.   Appeals should be heard by the Sheriff in chambers; the Sheriff would for this purpose be empowered to make such enquiries as he thought fit; to hear such persons (including the reporter and the child) as he thought fit; and the parent and any material witness whom he or she may desire to call should be given an opportunity of being heard.

113. If the Sheriff upholds such an appeal he should be required to state his reasons. He would then be empowered either to quash the order outright or to refer the case back to the panel for consideration, in the light of the judgment, of other methods of treatment.

114.   In our discussion of referral and appeal provisions we have throughout referred to "the Sheriff". In this context this term should be taken as including the Sheriff-Substitute.

115.   Under our proposals it is, we consider, desirable that there should be a right of appeal on questions of law, arising from proceedings before the Sheriff, to the Court of Session; and we recommend accordingly.

116.   Proceedings before the Sheriff will involve either disputed issues of fact (on referral at the outset) or appeals against measures authorised by the juvenile panels either initially or as a result of subsequent review. It seems to us important that, at either of these stages, involving as they may do decisions amounting to major interventions between parent and child, there should be a right of legal representation for any parent who desires it, and that for this purpose arrangements should be made for extension of State-assisted legal aid to persons who cannot afford to make their own arrangements for legal representation.

117.   In setting out these recommendations at some length, we are conscious that they may be in risk of conveying an impression of an unduly cumbersome if not unworkable machinery. If the result of our proposals were to be a duplication of hearings before the juvenile panels and the Sheriff, they would, we recognise, be unacceptable both on grounds of principle and practicability. We see no reason to fear such a result. Our proposals would on the one hand relieve the Sheriff Courts of some 90 per cent of the juvenile cases with which they are at present dealing. On the other hand, these courts would have to resolve disputed issues of fact in some juvenile cases which would formerly have been dealt with in juvenile courts other than the Sheriff Juvenile Court On the information before us, the total is unlikely to amount to more than 1,300 a

year, a fair number of which are in any event dealt with at present in the Sheriff Court. As to appeals, appeals against decisions of the juvenile courts are at present made to the High Court of Justiciary. The total number is relatively small, but even allowing for the effect of the new right of appeal to the Sheriff and the possibility that under the new arrangements there might initially be some increase in appeals, we see no reason to think that after the juvenile panels have been in operation for a limited period, the total volume would be markedly greater than at present. Moreover, in so far as appeals may be more likely against custodial orders, it should also be borne in mind that under our proposals (see paragraph 122), borstal and detention centre orders for juveniles beyond the age of 16 will continue to be made by the Sheriff Courts, and will thus to that extent not represent a new or added demand on the time of those courts.

CHAPTER VI

The Limits of the Juvenile Panels' Jurisdiction

THE UPPER AGE-LIMIT

118.   Under existing law the jurisdiction of the juvenile courts extends to children and young persons under the age of 17. In the light of the considerations discussed in Chapter III, it seems clear that, wherever drawn, the dividing line will to some extent be an arbitrary one, and indeed argument can be advanced for adopting any one of a variety of ages short of the age of 21, i.e., the age generally recognised as marking attainment of full adulthood. Below that age, the criminal law relating to juveniles already recognises a gradation of standards by drawing a distinction between "children", "young persons" and "young adults", i.e., those under 14, those between 14 and 17 and those between 17 and 21, though the practical effects—other than in relation to forms of custodial treatment—are fairly limited. The existing distinctions mark off those who may properly be described as children, and those within the age-range which includes those variously described in current usage as "adolescents", "young people" and "young adults". The problems involved in dealing with the higher age-groups seem to us to be quite different in character and degree from those arising from children's misbehaviour. The criminal law at present recognises the age of 14 as being the termination of "childhood"; and this is in keeping with the civil law, which has for centuries taken the dividing line as being the end of the state of pupillage (on attainment of the age of 14 (for boys) and 12 (for girls)), i.e., the period at which a child ceased to be regarded as in a state of tutelage under the control and direction of his or her parents. The latter principle seems to us to be essentially sound, and indeed reflects the criterion on which our proposals as a whole are based, namely, that the work of the juvenile panels stems basically from a preventive and educative principle. In every case where children in a state of tutelage, still undergoing compulsory education, appear before the panels, the question will in actual fact be one of special educational measures, the normal educational processes, whether in the home, the family environment or in the schools, having for whatever reason fallen short or failed in their effect. Accordingly, we recommend that the upper-age limit of the juvenile panels' jurisdiction should be related broadly to the age marking the end of compulsory full-time education. Generally speaking, this is at present 15, though, in view of the arrangements governing actual leaving dates, the school-

52

leaving age is in individual cases in practice often between the age of 15 and 16. The latter age is also the leaving age for pupils attending special schools, and it seems to us that as a matter of statutory provision the juvenile panels' jurisdiction should be extended to all children under the age of 16. (In the event of any future decision to raise the school leaving age beyond 15, we recognise that the upper age-limit of the juvenile panels' jurisdiction might need further consideration. The guiding factor in our view is the age-limit for full-time day school education.)

JURISDICTION IN RELATION TO YOUNG PEOPLE BETWEEN
THE AGES OF 16 AND 21

119.   Today, when young people on leaving school are increasingly enjoying an economic independence which is reflected in their leisure tastes, pursuits and mode of life generally, we see no purpose in continuing to draw distinction, for the purposes of procedure, between those between the ages of 16 and 17 (i.e., age 16–under 17) and those between 17 and 21. We therefore recommend that the age-group 16–21 should be regarded as a single intermediate group, who as a matter of procedure would be dealt with by the criminal courts of law under the normal criminal procedure applicable to adults. Summary jurisdiction in relation to young offenders between the ages of 16 and 21 would thus rest exclusively with the courts of summary jurisdiction (sitting in the normal way), and in consequence all existing juvenile courts would be abolished.

120.   We consider it desirable as a matter of procedure that it should be a statutory requirement that a social background report should be provided in every case (other than trivial) arising within this age-group, thus extending existing provision for social investigation to all young offenders under the age of 21.

121.   Our proposals may be felt to result in an unjustifiably drastic change in procedure at the age of 16. Below that age children will be dealt with under what is essentially part of the provision for educational measures: immediately thereafter they will be liable to be subjected to criminal procedure. We consider, however, that the effects can be exaggerated. The application of criminal procedure implies that the young people concerned have reached an age at which they can increasingly be expected to stand on their own feet and at which they have acquired a sufficient degree of maturity and understanding to enable them to assume responsibility for their actions. There has in recent times been much discussion about the extent to which the increasing physical maturity of young people and their increasing economic independence is matched by a corresponding degree of emotional maturity. We think that the gap, in so far as there is or may be one, has sometimes been exaggerated, and that, so far as emotional maturity is concerned, young people today compare by no means unfavourably with those of earlier generations, and that the processes of universal education (coupled with improved housing and public health standards) have already had effect. In any event, we do not think that it can be denied that this age-group are in actual fact largely an "autonomous generation". Where individual young people contravene the law, we see little purpose in subjecting them to a procedure which purports to treat them as children. Ultimately, the practical result will at that age, we think, depend less on the form of procedure than on the range of measures within the powers of the courts dealing with them. The application of criminal procedure will not, of course,

53

imply as a matter of treatment the application of the full sanctions of the criminal law appropriate to adults; we contemplate that the existing powers of disposal of the courts in relation to this age-group will remain broadly unchanged.

122. Two exceptions to that arise. With the lowering of the age-limit, already discussed, from 17 to 16, we recommend that the Secretary of State should take steps to make detention centre training (in practice at present virtually restricted to the Sheriff Court for the 17–21 age-group) available also for youths aged 16 to 17.

123. The preceding paragraphs relate to young offenders between the ages of 16 and 21. There remain a residual age-group of young people between the ages of 16 and 17 who may at present be the subject of "care or protection" proceedings. Any extension of this age-range seems on our earlier arguments unrealistic and unacceptable, and under our proposals we see little justification for retaining compulsory protective powers in relation to the 16–under 17 group. At present, the practical question in relation to this age-group arises only to a limited extent, and primarily in relation to girls, the question usually being one of moral danger. We have serious doubts whether at such an age, where the young women concerned may or may not be married and may already be mothers, any useful purpose is likely to be served by their appearance before the courts, which under our proposals will, so far as this age-group is concerned, be concerned almost exclusively with young offenders; nor for that matter does it seem appropriate to extend the powers of the juvenile panels, which will be dealing with what are essentially children's problems, to such an age-group. We are in any event not satisfied that matters of the kind in question involving persons of that age can, in the absence of actual criminal behaviour, appropriately be the subject of compulsory sanctions by a court of law.

Continuing Discretion of the Crown to Direct the Taking of Particular Cases Before a Criminal Court

124. Our broad proposal is that all juvenile offenders under the age of 16, subject only to very exceptional cases, should be referred to the juvenile panels. The jurisdiction of the present juvenile courts is subject to the qualification that the Lord Advocate may under common law direct the taking of particular cases, exceptionally and for grave reasons of public policy, in the Sheriff Court or for that matter in the High Court of Justiciary. In practice, directions affecting juveniles have been almost entirely confined to the gravest crimes such as murder, attempt to murder, culpable homicide, wounding with intent to cause grievous bodily harm, and rape. Road traffic offences, where conviction carries a liability to disqualification, have been directed to the Sheriff Court on the basis that the juvenile courts had no power of disqualification; and under the Road Traffic Act, 1962, the Sheriff Court is now the sole court of summary jurisdiction which may exercise this power.

125. We consider that the common law power of the Lord Advocate should continue to be applicable to juvenile offences. Its exercise would, we assume, arise only exceptionally and on the gravest crimes, in which major issues of public interest must necessarily arise, and in which, equally as a safeguard for the interests of the accused, trial under criminal procedure is essential.

126. We do not consider it desirable to attempt to restrict the existing Crown discretion, which has for long been a basic feature of our system of criminal

procedure and which, we believe, commands general public confidence. Our sole qualification relates to road traffic offences by juveniles. We see no reason in principle why such cases, involving children under 16, should not be dealt with in future by the juvenile panels. It would in our view be inappropriate to invest the panels with a power to order disqualification. Such cases seem likely to be comparatively few. If it is felt to be a matter of practical importance that the power to order disqualification should remain in respect of children of this age, the situation could, we think, be met under our proposals by making provision under which, on an order being made by the panel, the case would automatically be intimated by the reporter to the procurator fiscal. The latter would then be empowered to report the case to the Sheriff Court, which, if it thought fit, could order disqualification.

TERRITORIAL JURISDICTION OF THE JUVENILE PANELS

127.   In the great majority of cases, the measures instituted by the juvenile panels will involve the child's supervision within the community, i.e., in his home area. In a number of cases, however, the facts or circumstances occasioning the referral will arise outwith the child's home area, and in some the child's home area may initially be in doubt. A juvenile panel anywhere should, therefore, be empowered to assume interim jurisdiction for the purpose of inquiries in relation to any child brought before it on a referral by the reporter; to make interim custodial orders; and to transfer the case to another area on the latter being established as the child's home area. Any interim order should at that stage be subject to confirmation or variation, or substitution by a permanent order by the "home area" panel. The foregoing comments relate to cases in which there are no disputed issues of fact relating to the grounds of referral. Where on appearance before the panel such disputes arise (and would under our proposals thus be referred to the Sheriff), we contemplate that the referral would be to the Sheriff Court having jurisdiction in the area in which the facts and circumstances grounding the referral arose, irrespective of whether or not this was the child's home area. If the Sheriff upheld the referral, the case would then be remitted to the "home area" juvenile panel for consideration of treatment measures in the normal way.

DEFINITION OF THE BASIS OF THE JUVENILE PANELS' JURISDICTION

128.   We have already indicated that the children (under 16) coming within the juvenile panels' jurisdiction would be all those whose need for special measures of education and training was such as could be met only on the basis of public intervention. For the purposes of statutory definition of the range of cases coming within the panels' jurisdiction, we draw attention to the following matters:

(a) Juveniles in need of care or protection
Section 65(1)(a) of the 1937 Act defines this class as including—

> a child or young person who, having no parent or guardian or a parent or guardian unfit to exercise care and guardianship or not exercising proper care and guardianship, is falling into bad associations or exposed to moral danger, or beyond control; ... and who, in any such case as aforesaid, requires care or protection;

It will be seen that this definition is such as to require positive evidence of two factors—(*a*) facts or circumstances postulating a need for "care or protection" and (*b*) an absence, of, or failure in, parental control.

129. It was represented to us that in certain cases the second factor may be extremely difficult to prove. The facts and circumstances may well be such as to show, on any reasonable criterion, a clear and urgent need for measures of care and training. It may, however, be extremely difficult to establish, e.g., in the case of a 15-year-old girl who persistently runs away from home, that there is in fact a failure in parental control. The difficulties seem to us to be essentially similar to those which we have discussed in Chapter I (in relation to parental responsibility and the imposition of fines on parents). In the latter situation it is under existing arrangements already accepted that it would be impracticable to place any positive requirement on the prosecution or the court to satisfy itself affirmatively as to lack of parental control. In "care or protection" proceedings, we consider that the existing standards as to the matters on which positive evidence has to be adduced—apart from the element of lack of parental control—are already stringent. It seems to us that the test should in each case be the child's present need for protective measures, and that it is placing an unduly restrictive, and unrealistic, burden on the petitioner to seek to require positive proof of lack of parental control. We recommend, therefore, that in the legal definition of the future equivalent of "care or protection", reference to the question of parental control should be omitted. On that basis the parents' general circumstances would continue to be one of the matters before the juvenile panels, and would, of course, be a relevant matter in deciding, where the need for special educational measures was established, the nature of the measures to be applied, e.g., in deciding whether to make a custodial order as opposed to a supervision order.

(b) Refractory children beyond parental control

130. Section 68 of the 1937 Act empowers a parent to bring his child before a juvenile court on the ground that the child is beyond his control. It was represented to us that, rare though such situations may be, it was most undesirable that parents should be able to put themselves in the position of "prosecutor" against their own children, and that, while in extreme situations the child's removal from home might be necessary, such action should be instituted by some person or agency other than the parent. Under our proposals we would hope that the need for action of this kind before the juvenile panels would be even rarer than at present. The parents would, we assume, in most cases have already been in touch with the social education department (either direct or as a result of an approach to the "reporter") and measures would have resulted by agreement whereby advice and guidance would be made available through a child guidance clinic or other specialist agency. Where, exceptionally, an order by the juvenile panel was considered necessary, we contemplate that action would as in any other instance be at the hand of the reporter on the basis of reports made to him by the social education department. In these circumstances the power of the parent himself to bring the child before the panel would seem to us unnecessary, and we recommend that the existing provision should in this respect be repealed.

(c) Truancy and unreasonable failure to attend school

131. Under the Education (Scotland) Act, 1962, every parent has a duty to secure his child's attendance at school while the child is within the age for compulsory education. Unreasonable failure to comply with the provision is an offence punishable in the case of repeated failure with fine or imprisonment (or both). In practice, before prosecution is contemplated, discussions normally take place between the school, the education authority or one of its committees or sub-committees (frequently a school management committee) and the parents. If these fail, an attendance order may be served on the parent, against which he has a right of appeal to the Sheriff. A prosecution against the parents is normally instituted only where all these steps have failed. On a parent's conviction the court may (and shall if the education authority so require) direct that the child should be brought before a juvenile court, and in such circumstances the juvenile court may make any order which it has power to make in the case of a child or young person in need of "care or protection". The education authority is also empowered—whether or not proceedings are taken against the parent— to bring the child before a juvenile court.

132. It was represented to us that the various steps provided for under existing legislation sometimes result in lengthy delays which can only be prejudicial to the child; that this arises more particularly where these matters are handled by school management committees, which deal with the matter only as one of a variety of unrelated functions; and that there is understandably often a reluctance on the part of such a committee to authorise steps for the institution of a prosecution.

133. Failure to attend school regularly (including persistent truancy) may be due to a variety of causes, and under our proposals we consider it appropriate that all cases, where compulsory action on these grounds is in issue, should from the outset be referred to the juvenile panel. In many it may then be possible to decide on appropriate action with the agreement of the parents. Given the nature of the juvenile panels as we conceive them, there appears to be no useful purpose in a continuance of the present arrangements for preliminary consideration of these cases by the education authority or one of its committees. Unreasonable failure to attend school would under our recommendations become one of the grounds on which a child could be brought before the juvenile panels in the same way as any of the other classes of children requiring special educational measures, namely, at the instance of the panel's reporter.

134. The paramount question in every case must be the child's interests, and this can in our view best be considered on a referral to the juvenile panel. Under our proposals we contemplate that the great majority of cases will be dealt with in this way, and that the question of prosecuting the parents in the criminal courts will in practice thus rarely arise. We cannot, however, rule out the latter possibility entirely; situations (fortunately comparatively rare) may continue to occur in which it is clear that the child is being unreasonably withheld from school by the wilful action of his parents. Infrequent though such cases may be, parental action of this kind, which is already recognised as tantamount to criminal neglect, should clearly continue to be subject to the sanctions of the law; and the power under the 1962 Act to take proceedings against parents in such circumstances should continue to be available as a measure of last resort for breach of their statutory obligation to secure their children's education.

(d) Other situations involving the compulsory application of special measures of education and training

135.   Two other statutory provisions seem to us to call for amendment. Under the Education (Scotland) Act, 1962, education authorities have a duty to ascertain what children in their areas, because of mental or physical disability, require special educational treatment or are unable to benefit from education and should be referred to the local health authority. At the time of the initial decision that a child falls into either category the parent has a right of appeal to the Secretary of State; in the case of a child referred to the local health authority there is provision for a further appeal to the Secretary of State after at least a year has elapsed. In either of these situations, involving the application of compulsory measures, it seems to us entirely appropriate, under our proposals, that in the event of disagreement between the education authority and the parents, the matter should be resolved by the juvenile panel (and not the Secretary of State) on the basis of a referral by the reporter acting on a report from the director of social education.

136.   Secondly, under sections 2–4 of the Children Act, 1948, children received into the care of local authorities may in certain circumstances later be made the subject of a resolution by the local authority which has the effect of vesting parental rights over the child in that authority. Section 4 provides for appeal against such a resolution to the Sheriff. Under our proposals, it is appropriate that appeal against such action should be made to the juvenile panel (the issue again being simply another instance of compulsory measures involving deprivation of parental rights).

137.   In both situations, the panels' decisions would, as in any other case referred to them, be subject to the general right of appeal to the Sheriff, already discussed.

Definition

138.   We have already made it clear that, in our view, referral should be made to juvenile panels for one reason only, namely, that *prima facie* the child is in need of special measures of education and training. In the light of what is said above, we consider that the panels should be empowered to assume jurisdiction to order such measures for any child under 16 in respect of whom, on a referral, one or more of the following circumstances is shown to apply, namely, his falling into bad associations or exposure to moral danger; his being the subject of criminal neglect or an unnatural offence (or being within the same household as such a child); his having violated the law as to crimes and offences; his being beyond control; his failure to attend school (whether by reason of truancy or parental refusal to comply with a requirement by the education authority of attendance at a particular school); his parent or guardian having abandoned him or suffering from some permanent disability rendering him incapable of caring for the child, or who is of such habits or mode of life as to be unfit to have the care of the child.

139.   At this stage it may be helpful to summarise our proposals as follows:

(1)   (*a*)   subject to the overriding discretion of the Crown (to be exercised exceptionally and for grave reasons of public policy) to prosecute in the

Sheriff Court or the High Court of Justiciary, all juveniles under 16 should in principle be removed from the jurisdiction of the criminal courts;

(*b*) instead, juvenile panels should have power, on the grounds set out in paragraph 138, to assume jurisdiction over juveniles under 16 and to order special measures of education and training according to the needs of the juvenile concerned;

(*c*) disputed issues of fact relating to the grounds for assuming jurisdiction should be automatically referred to the Sheriff; and orders made by the panels should be subject to a right of appeal to the Sheriff;

(2) all existing juvenile courts should be abolished;

(3) the ordinary courts of summary jurisdiction should be the sole courts of summary jurisdiction in relation to young offenders between the ages of 16 and 21;

(4) provision for "care or protection" proceedings in relation to young people aged 16 and over should be abolished;

(5) any rule of law or statutory provision establishing a minimum age of criminal responsibility should be repealed.

CHAPTER VII

The Powers of the Juvenile Panels—Non-Residential Measures of Supervision within the Community

SUPERVISION, FORMAL AND INFORMAL

140. We have already made it clear in Chapter IV that the juvenile panel's basic action, on being satisfied that ground for intervention exists, will be to assume oversight of the child, that oversight, as a practical matter, being carried out on their behalf by the social education department. We now go on to consider, in more detail, the practical measures of treatment available to the panels. These, as we have already described them in outline, essentially represent the application of a process of social education, which in the great majority of cases will be carried on while the child remains within the home, but which will sometimes involve his removal from home for temporary periods for more specialised and intensive residential training. Wherever possible the aim must be to strengthen and develop the natural influences for good within the home and family, and likewise to assist the parents in overcoming factors adverse to the child's sound and normal up-bringing. Our proposals will, we consider, result in a substantially greater use of community measures of case-work with children on the lines of the present probation, or of supervision under the 1937 Act, the case-work being carried out most commonly, under the juvenile panel's authority, by the social work staff of the social education department which we are recommending. One necessary consequence of our proposals is that the present distinction between supervision under the 1937 Act and probation as methods of treatment for juveniles would cease to exist. Probation as such is a method of treatment which has from the outset necessarily evolved in the closest association with the criminal courts. As such, it will, of

59

course, continue in relation to persons dealt with by the criminal courts, but can of necessity have no place under the arrangements for the juvenile panels which we are recommending. We discuss the practical consequences, in terms of reorganisation of local social services, in Chapter XII.

141.   Referral to the panel will be at the instance of the panel's reporter, but it is obvious that the reports leading to such action may emanate from a wide variety of public and voluntary agencies, including the police. Moreover, in any given case any one or other of these agencies may have an important part to play not merely in the identification of the individual child in need, but equally in the separate and subsequent stages involving assessment of these needs and the measures to be applied as a result. When we say that supervision will most commonly be entrusted to the social education service, we by no means imply that this task will never be entrusted to other social agencies, public or voluntary. On the contrary, there may well be situations in which one or other of these is already in close contact with the home, and could more appropriately undertake the child's supervision. What is, however, vitally important is that the social education department should be recognised as having general oversight on behalf of the panel and as the central focal point of information and co-ordination of action. This will under our proposals automatically result on any case being the subject of formal referral to the juvenile panel, but it is equally important that similar arrangements should exist, where, as we contemplate, informal supervision measures (not involving prior referral to the panel) are instituted. The work done by the police in particular in these directions at present is not, we think, widely understood, and we think that it may be helpful to indicate their present role in this respect and under the new arrangements as we envisage them in the future.

THE ROLE OF THE POLICE

142.   The established principle under the Scottish system of public prosecution is that, while acts recognised by the criminal law as crimes or offences carry a liability to prosecution, the decision whether or not to institute proceedings in any particular case is vested in an independent public prosecutor. It is not perhaps generally appreciated that this discretion brings the prosecutor, who is normally considered to be more concerned with quasi-judicial functions, directly into the field of treatment. A decision not to prosecute has effect in the field of treatment in that, where there is no prosecution, there is no opportunity for the application of compulsory treatment measures. This consideration is clearly an important one. One possible result is that prosecution may be waived, on the view that the knowledge that he has been detected in the offence is in itself in certain circumstances likely to have a sufficient effect on the offender. In some cases, the prosecutor may couple such a decision with a decision to warn the offender orally or in writing; and may either do so himself or instruct the police to do so on his behalf.

143.   Not all police warnings are administered at the explicit instructions of the prosecutor. Warnings may be given to offenders of any age and the practice has, of course, for long been adopted fairly widely for juvenile offenders. In this way, the police can be seen to be—from the standpoint of juvenile delinquency, an executive agency administering a particular form of treatment. They are also, of

course, and will remain, because of their functions in crime detecting, one of the primary sources of identification of children in need of special educational measures; as well as being part of the sifting or assessment agency.

144.   Within this general framework, the police have, of course, always and necessarily exercised some measure of discretion. The wide range of actions which may amount to common law or statutory offences, and their relative gravity or triviality in the particular circumstances of the case, makes it inevitable that in practice the individual constable in the course of his normal duty must exercise some measure of discretion, and equally that, even where individual offenders are reported by the individual constable, the Chief Constable or his senior officers will in certain cases decide not to report to the prosecutor. The origins of the system of police warnings are perhaps best illustrated by the example of the village constable, who in earlier times was very much a "guide, philosopher and friend", who knew his clientele, and who was in a position to judge those occasions on which an informal word of caution was the appropriate remedy. The system of "juvenile warnings" as normally understood, nowadays, however, implies a somewhat greater degree of formality, i.e., warning on appearance before the Chief Constable or a senior police officer. The latter arrangement, which was reviewed and commended by the Scottish Advisory Council on the Treatment and Rehabilitation of Offenders in their report on this subject,* seems to us to represent essentially a development of what has from the earliest times been a feature inherent in police duty—a development more particularly applicable to urban areas, where contact between the police and individual members of the public is necessarily on a more impersonal footing.

145.   The essence of the juvenile warnings procedure as indicated in the S.A.C.T.R.O. Report, already referred to, is that it is informal and voluntary. Its exercise arises only where the police have adequate evidence of the guilt of the offender and it rests on an invitation to the parents to attend at a police station at an arranged time with their child where, with their consent and in their presence, he is orally warned by the Chief Constable or a senior police officer. The procedure is thus entirely dependent on the co-operation and consent of the parents, and the preliminary explanation given to them carries—and in our view should carry—no suggestion or implication whatsoever as to possible police action in the event of their withholding their agreement. The decision at that stage is, and must remain, entirely the parents'. Further, the procedure is in general invoked only in relation to first offenders.

146.   The evidence which we have received suggested that these arrangements met with widespread approval and, apart from the few minor matters discussed in paragraph 148, we do not suggest that they need any appreciable alteration. It would, we think, be generally conceded that much juvenile delinquency, particularly among younger children, consists of acts of petty mischief which do not require elaborate or sustained treatment measures; and that, in so far as they do need to be dealt with by public action, they can very appropriately be met by means of warning. Indeed, as we have indicated in earlier paragraphs, we consider that, in future, warning at the instance of the juvenile panels will be a relatively infrequent occurrence. It seems to us that if in the future it is agreed

---

* "Police Warnings": Report of Scottish Advisory Council on the Treatment and Rehabilitation of Offenders, 1945

by all those officially concerned in the preliminary sifting process that the appropriate outcome is in fact a warning, then formal referral to the panels is in most cases likely to be unnecessary. Warning to be effective should be given expeditiously, and we see no need in such cases to set in train the more elaborate machinery of referral to the panel. In saying this we are not unmindful that what may outwardly appear to be minor offences may on occasion prove to be in fact the symptoms of more serious underlying emotional disturbance. The risk of such situations arising in relation to the type of cases in which police warnings are at present given seems to us to be extremely remote. Moreover, in so far as there may in future be an extension of the police juvenile liaison scheme to other areas (a matter which we discuss in paragraphs 149–156), we contemplate that this will be supported by a growing element of relatively simple training whereby the police officers most directly concerned will have the necessary skills and insights to be alert to such possibilities, and thus to bring them to the attention of an appropriate social agency.

147. No preliminary sifting instrument can guarantee absolute success. We understand, however, that of juveniles dealt with by police warning about 90 per cent do not come into police hands again. Even were it arguable that at least some of those concerned would have reacted similarly without a warning, we consider that this figure, bearing in mind that it relates to several thousand warnings annually (in 1962, over 4,000) must on any reasonable criterion be regarded as an indicator of the efficacy of the system as a whole. With co-operation and consultation between the police and the social education department we think that even this high standard might be improved.

148. The evidence before us indicated that the vast majority of Scottish police forces operate a warnings system in accordance with the S.A.C.T.R.O. recommendation. The exceptions are a few county forces serving areas where the need for such a system is in any event limited, and in which juveniles are no doubt cautioned by the local constable in the normal course of duty. In these areas, we understand that cases reported up through police channels to the Chief Constable are always referred by him to the appropriate public prosecutor; in these forces we are inclined to think, notwithstanding the factors already mentioned, that there may still be scope for the introduction of the more formal system of juvenile warnings by the Chief Constable or a senior officer. We also understand, that—a few areas apart—where a public prosecutor himself decides on a juvenile warning he does not administer it himself, but instructs the police to do so. We think that there are advantages in all juvenile warnings being given by a single authority, readily recognisable as such to children, namely, the police. Under our proposals, we contemplate that this procedure would be followed generally in relation to warnings decided upon by the reporter to the juvenile panel.

POLICE JUVENILE LIAISON SCHEMES

149. The police juvenile liaison scheme represents an extension of the police warning system in that warning is followed in appropriate cases by a period of informal supervision by a specially selected police officer, the Juvenile Liaison Officer, or, in larger forces, one of his team of officers. Supervision is carried out by visits to the child's home, school and minister or priest. Visits to schools and clergymen are made with the consent of parents. Efforts are made to enlist the child's active co-operation, and to persuade him to join a youth organisation

near his home. Parents are encouraged to discuss their problems with the officers concerned and in appropriate cases attempts are made to help in finding suitable employment for older children.

150. The juvenile liaison scheme was first introduced in the City of Liverpool in 1949, and placed on a firm basis in 1952. The work of the Liverpool scheme is well described in the publication entitled, "The Police and Children", an extract from which, describing the scheme in more detail, is set out in Appendix C. We have had the advantage of discussing the Liverpool arrangements at first hand with the Chief Constable and officers of his juvenile liaison staff, and have also received full information about similar schemes in Scotland which have more recently been instituted in Greenock, Stirlingshire and Clackmannan, and Coatbridge. The schemes have since been extended to three other Scottish police forces (Kilmarnock, Paisley and Perth).

151. Somewhat different arrangements with essentially the same purpose have operated in the City of Aberdeen since 1936. Informal supervision in appropriate cases which are the subject of police warning is carried out by the probation service by agreement with the Chief Constable, after discussion of each case between the principal probation officer and a senior police officer. On the information before us, the results of both schemes have been highly encouraging, although we recognise that the Scottish juvenile liaison schemes have not as yet been in operation for a lengthy period. We also record that comment on the schemes by a fairly wide variety of Scottish witnesses was, with certain exceptions, favourable, though there was apparently some division of view among the police themselves as to the appropriateness of their undertaking supervision of this kind. Such opposition as was expressed appeared to us to be based largely on theoretical considerations and in some cases without full first-hand knowledge of the operation of the schemes. The arguments of principle and practice against the schemes seemed to us to rest essentially on three points, (*a*) that the application of supervision measures should in all cases be by order of a juvenile court (or any other public authority that might take its place), (*b*) that the work went beyond the scope of police duties, and (*c*) that the police were not trained for such work.

152. As the discussion in the preceding paragraphs indicates, however, the exercise of a measure of discretion in referrals has for long been an inherent—and in our view commendable—feature of the Scottish system of public prosecution. We appreciate that the view has been taken in some quarters that the institution of juvenile courts, with greater assessment facilities, makes it appropriate that the application of treatment measures should in every case be decided by such courts. For our part we do not accept that view as applying either to juvenile courts as at present constituted or to the juvenile panels which we are recommending. Under our proposals, assuming that he is satisfied that grounds for intervention exist, the issue confronting the reporter to the panel will in every case be whether the child requires treatment of a kind such as to justify formal referral to the panel, as distinct from informal measures. In other words, the issue is essentially how best to treat the needs of the child, and whether this aim would be furthered, or could be attained only, by a formal referral to the panel. Nor are we able to accept the argument as to the nature of police duties. Police duty can never be static, and it seems to us that police juvenile liaison is no more than an attempt to apply, in changing urban

conditions, principles which have always been and are still being carried out in a less formal way in course of police duty, more particularly in rural areas. Indeed the schemes seem to us primarily appropriate for urban areas. It also seemed to us that, among those urban police forces which have not so far adopted schemes, opposition to them was not uniformly strong. In at least one area it appeared that local attitudes were influenced by the fact that the police had in earlier years—prior to the introduction of the present statutory service—acted as probation officers, and in that area the police were, in the absence of some more definite measure of official approval, reluctant to extend their activities into this sphere.

153. It was also suggested that the police were not trained to undertake this type of work and had not the necessary skills to identify cases in which the underlying problems were such as to require more intensive treatment measures by an experienced social worker. This view appears to us, however, to be based on certain misapprehensions. From an early stage of the introduction of such schemes in Scotland arrangements have been developed, in association with the Departments of Social Study and Psychological Medicine in the University of Glasgow, for a periodic series of group discussions (involving both theoretical and practical subjects) which are attended by officers from all existing Scottish juvenile liaison units. These courses are, we understand, likely to be developed further and should, we think, go far to ensure that all concerned are operating within a unified and informed framework of approach. They are, however, not intended to provide social work training, but simply to enable the police officers concerned to play an informed part in identifying signs of more serious trouble calling for specialist skills.

154. The efficient working of the schemes seems to us to depend in large measure on the quality of the officers concerned and the inspiration given by their superiors. Not all areas may have an equal need for such schemes, and we would not wish to suggest that the juvenile liaison schemes as at present operating are the only or the final pattern of organisation which might emerge. In some areas, notably in Aberdeen, different arrangements, dependent largely on the nature of the area and local organisation and local personalities, appear to work equally well.

155. In short, it seems to us that the existing juvenile liaison schemes are serving a most useful purpose. We commend the valuable and devoted work already being done, and recommend their extension to other urban areas. It would in our view be undesirable to attempt to place such schemes on a mandatory statutory basis. The schemes must in our view remain permissive. Their detailed form may well vary from area to area; and it seems to us that there is a place not only for the existing schemes, including that in Aberdeen, but for other possible local experiments, which are to be encouraged. We mention, as one example brought to our notice in this connection, the work already being done in the wider field of delinquency prevention by the City of Nottingham Police in association with local schools (an outline of which is given in Appendix D). Such experiments in the development of good police–public relationships, particularly with juveniles, seem to us to have an important part to play in the prevention of crime.

156. The evidence which we received led us to believe that co-operation between the police and the schools, and between the police and various other

social services concerned with children's problems, in certain areas fell short of what is desirable. On the one hand, it seems clear that there are many occasions in which, were they to be approached informally by the police, headmasters and teachers could often do much to assist where signs of incipient delinquency are developing. Conversely, in some areas police activity in this sphere tends to be regarded with reserve, partly on the view that the police are in danger of undertaking duties thought to be appropriate to trained social workers. Those responsible for the operation of juvenile liaison schemes made it clear to us that they are fully alive to this problem; the purpose of the Glasgow courses already mentioned is, as we have indicated, in no sense intended to train the police juvenile liaison staff as social workers, but to enable them to play an informed and responsible role in the diagnostic or preliminary sifting process, so that cases beyond their capacity can immediately be referred to agencies competent to deal with them. There will always be cases in which the police juvenile liaison approach will be particularly appropriate and to which certain children will respond readily. Under our proposals, such schemes will continue to play an important part. There is, we believe, already a growing awareness within the police service and the social services concerned that each has a distinctive contribution in this field, and that their common objective demands that there should be the closest co-operation between them at all levels. Our recommendations for reorganisation of the latter services will, we think, assist that process, and we contemplate that under our own proposals, there would in practice be the closest co-operation and understanding between the Chief Constable, the reporter to the panel, and the director of social education in questions of general policy relating to informal methods of police supervision; and, at day-to-day working level, between police juvenile liaison officers and officers of the social education department.

THE SCOPE OF FORMAL SUPERVISION ORDERS

157.   In making a supervision order, the juvenile panel should in our view have the widest discretion to include in it any of the conditions which may at present be included in a supervision order or probation order. Because of the greater informality of proceedings before the panel it would, we think, no doubt be possible for the panel to apply, formally or otherwise, a variety of unorthodox conditions if it appeared to it that these would be beneficial in particular cases. The conditions could incorporate in a less formal way the "attendance" idea, i.e., attendance at some centre where the child would be encouraged to undertake socially useful work. This would, however, be done on what would be essentially a voluntary basis, and would not be linked in any way with compulsory attendance at an attendance centre. There will be limits to the lengths to which the idea of inserting formal conditions in a supervision order can be carried by the panels themselves; much can probably be done in this way by a supervising officer in the course of supervision, and in so far as measures of this kind were applied by the panels, we would assume that they would do so only on the recommendation of, or after consultation with, the officer who was to be the supervisor.

158.   Under existing arrangements juveniles (whether regarded as delinquents or as being in need of "care or protection") may be committed to the care of a "fit person" (including a local authority). The effect of such an order is to vest parental rights over the child in the "fit person", and the child may either be

placed with an individual "fit person" or, as more commonly happens, be placed in public care with a local authority (which by administrative action results in placing with foster parents or in a children's home). Under our proposals, the need for a separate legal provision of this kind will disappear. The juvenile panel's action will in these circumstances be to place the child under the oversight of the social education department, with the additional requirement that he should be accommodated under whatever appear to be the most appropriate arrangements, whether under public care or under the care of a recognised voluntary agency. As a result, while the child will in all day-to-day matters be looked after either by foster parents or within a children's home, legal jurisdiction over the child will continue to rest with the juvenile panel, exercising continuing oversight through the director of social education.

FINDING OF CAUTION

159.   Finding of caution by parents for their child's good behaviour may in certain circumstances be a useful measure. This is a contingent liability, which calls for constructive effort on the part of the parents. It may be that at present it may in some circumstances work unduly harshly in that the parents' efforts may fail through no observable fault of their own, or alternatively because, through constitutional defects, the parents' efforts though the best they can muster are not good enough. Under our proposals, we recommend accordingly that the juvenile panels should have power to order finding of caution by the parents, but we contemplate that such a finding would normally be coupled with a supervision order placing the child under the supervision of the social education department, so that the full facts would be before the panel before any question of forfeiture, or sanctions in event of failure to find caution, arose.

FORMAL WARNINGS BY THE PANEL

160.   In general, we should expect that in practice considerably fewer cases would be dealt with simply by warning or admonition on appearance before the panel, either because (as we have indicated) more warnings would be given informally, or because where there was an appearance, warning would be coupled more frequently with formal or informal supervision measures. A number of witnesses criticised the perfunctory and unimpressive way in which warnings were given in some courts; clearly a warning should be so given as to be unmistakenly recognised as such by the recipient.

CASES IN WHICH NO ACTION IS DIRECTED

161.   Situations will no doubt occasionally arise in which the panels are satisfied that while the grounds of action (involving some relatively minor legal infringement) have been made out, there is nevertheless, in the light of the whole circumstances, no occasion for special treatment measures (except in so far as the fact of appearance before the panel itself may have had a beneficial effect). In these situations, the panel would simply make no order and discharge the case. Since, in the referral of cases to the panel by the reporter, the test would be primarily whether the child's needs were likely to be furthered, and could be attained only, by formal referral to the panel, such situations would in practice be unlikely to arise frequently.

162. Several of our witnesses recommended the introduction in Scotland of attendance centres. The Criminal Justice Act, 1948, provided for the setting up of such centres in England and Wales, the provision being introduced at a comparatively late stage of the Bill's enactment. At that time it was, we understand, considered inappropriate against that background and in the absence of practical experience of such centres, to make any comparable provision in the corresponding Scottish measure of 1949.

163. As now developed in England and Wales, the attendance centre system is governed by the following main features—

(a) attendance at such a centre may be ordered for any juvenile aged 10 and under 21 who is found guilty of an offence punishable in the case of an adult with imprisonment;

(b) attendance may be ordered for periods up to a maximum of 24 hours and not less than 12 hours; attendance usually being on alternate Saturdays for sessions of 2 hours each;

(c) over fifty centres for boys under 17 have been provided, held in schools, youth club premises and police premises such as training schools (away from police stations). Part of each session is devoted to physical education and the remainder to handicrafts, gardening work and some talks on subjects such as citizenship or first-aid;

(d) the centres are staffed by police officers who undertake this work in what would otherwise be their free time, payment for their services being made at rates appropriate to instructors in local institutions;

(e) an experimental centre for youths of 17–21 has been operating at Manchester since 1958 and is staffed by officers from the local prison.

164. The operation of English attendance centres was fairly recently reviewed by the Home Secretary's Advisory Council on the Treatment of Offenders.* They concluded that the centres had a useful role and that their further extension in urban areas was desirable. In the evidence which they had received, criticism had, they indicated, been made that the period of attendance was too short and that the intervals between the attendances were too long; that the training provided was not constructive enough, and that it should in any event be followed up by a period of after-care. In their view, however, at least some of these criticisms were based on a misunderstanding of the centres' purpose, and they drew attention to the published findings reached by a research inquiry carried out by the Cambridge Institute of Criminology, which were "that attendance centres are quite effective when applied to a young offender with little or no experience of crime, coming from a fairly normal home background; but, when applied to the recidivist with two or more previous offences, especially one who has already failed to respond to probation, the results are not at all encouraging". In other words, the attendance centre is a satisfactory method of dealing with a strictly limited class of young delinquents—those whose minds are still open to the effect of punishment by deprivation of leisure, and the influence of the attendance centre staff in teaching them to respect the law and the property of others. The Council's conclusion was that, judged by that standard, the centres appeared to have achieved a fair measure of success.

---

* "Non-Residential Treatment of Offenders under 21": Report by the Advisory Council on Treatment of Offenders, 1962.

165. We have carefully considered the matter in the light of the English Council's findings and the evidence we have received. Some of us have also been afforded facilities for visiting some of the English centres and of seeing something of their work at first hand.

166. We doubt whether in Scotland it would ever be practicable to set up more than a few such centres in the principal urban areas. It seems to us that the attendance centre system has a useful, if limited, part to play in the treatment of juvenile delinquency. We recommend that centres should be set up on the basis indicated, and consider that they should be made available for boys under the age of 16. We do not feel that under our proposals it would be appropriate that the centres should be staffed by police officers, a view which was shared in the evidence given before us by the Chief Constables' (Scotland) Association. In saying this, we in no way wish to cast doubt on the valuable, and indeed devoted, work being done in the existing centres in England by police officers. Under our own proposals we can, however, see no cogent argument for this work being undertaken by the police, and we recommend that the centres should be set up and financed by the education authority and run by the social education department which we are recommending. In view of the strictly limited purpose of the attendance centre, which is of course essentially a non-residential form of treatment, we do not consider that it should be accompanied by any form of continuing supervision. If supervision is appropriate, we think that this should be applied from the outset. In practice, a supervision order will often include a requirement that the child should attend at the supervisor's office, and children under supervision may often on a voluntary basis be introduced to youth clubs and other constructive social activities. This is, however, essentially different from compulsory attendance at an attendance centre, and we do not think that the two methods should be confused.

CHAPTER VIII

Residential Measures, and the Juvenile Panels' Powers to Order Residential Treatment

PRELIMINARY OBSERVATIONS

167. In the preceding chapters we have discussed the range of powers which we recommend should be available to the juvenile panels to order supervision, care and training within the community. We now consider the provision which should be made for residential measures involving the child's removal from the home and parental control, whether for short or longer periods. There has hitherto been a tendency to distinguish such measures fairly sharply from those involving supervision within the community. While this distinction may be a very real one from the point of view of its effects both on the parent and the child, viewed objectively as part of the training measures adapted to the individual child's needs it becomes less apparent. The residential measures in question amount to no more than a period of intensive and specialised "in-treatment" for what is usually a limited period. Throughout the period of residential training there should, it seems to us, be the closest contact with the

68

staff of the social education department concerned, who will have reported on the child before the period of residential training was decided upon, and under whose supervision the child may already have been at an earlier stage. These officers should in our view throughout maintain contact with the child's home in preparation for his eventual return. In that way the period of residential training would be seen simply as a continuation of an existing process, to be followed naturally by a return to the same supervising agency on the child's release into the community. The existing arrangements, owing to the variety and division of statutory functions over the whole field of treatment of children, and the separate services created as a result, seem to us to militate unnecessarily against that continuity of treatment.

168.   The difficulties arising under existing arrangements can perhaps best be illustrated by practical example. A fair number of the witnesses who appeared before us commented on the subject of approved schools. It was, for example, said that children under 12 should never be sent to approved schools; that delinquents and "care or protection" cases should never be in the same school; that too many children are sent to approved schools unnecessarily; that approved schools should be reserved for those above general school-leaving age; and that, more generally, too many cases unsuitable for approved schools are being sent there. More generally, the situation revealed in our discussions can, as the witnesses agreed, be described as follows :

(*a*)   there appears to be an insufficient range and variety of schools within the present approved school system;

(*b*)   there is a shortage of hospital accommodation for children suffering from mental defect;

(*c*)   there is a need for residential schools for children suffering from serious maladjustment or from educable mental handicap—and approved schools as at present established can be expected to cater for only a limited number of such cases;

(*d*)   there are inadequacies within the local authority child care field in that in some cases committal to approved school, though recognised as far from ideal, has to be resorted to as inevitable in the absence of a wider range of residential facilities within the sphere of children's homes provided by or available to the local authority;

(*e*)   there is a need for short-term residential training facilities (the witnesses here usually linking their proposals with suggestions as to the need for junior detention centres and the inadequacy of remand home detention as a method of treatment).

169.   While no quantitative evidence is readily available on these matters, the views expressed reflect the practical experience of a wide variety of professional witnesses in the education, child care, medical and approved school fields. The fact that there appears to be a general awareness of these problems in such circles, many of which could at least in theory be remedied by the exercise of existing statutory powers of local authorities (under one statutory arm or another) seems to us to reflect (*a*) the effects of lack of a unifying principle within the existing services concerned with education and child welfare; (*b*) a tendency in some quarters to regard children coming before the courts—at any rate delinquents—as a class apart; and (*c*) problems (financial and other) affected by the size and number of local authorities.

170. Some of the difficulties mentioned relate to local authority children's homes provided for children received into care under the Children Act, 1948. Reception into care in these cases is normally carried out by informal process, and the majority of the children have not appeared before the juvenile courts. They are, of course, received into public care either because they are homeless or because of disturbed home conditions. In the majority of cases involving long-term care, it is possible to place many of the children with foster parents or for adoption. Children received into public care in this way are, however, likely to show in greater or lesser degree some measure of emotional disturbance, and for this and other reasons a substantial number are cared for in children's homes. The extent of maladjustment or emotional disturbance shows a wide variation from case to case, and where present in its more serious forms, the presence of even a limited number of such children in a children's home can undoubtedly create serious practical problems. At present it may in extreme cases even result, in the absence of other more suitable provision, in steps being taken for the child's committal to an approved school, with resultant difficulties in turn in the schools.

171. We understand that several local authorities and voluntary bodies at present maintain children's homes which in practice are recognised as to some extent making more specialised provision for maladjusted and seriously disturbed children in care. The evidence before us, however, suggested that the facilities available were limited to certain areas, and that even in those homes the staffing standards sometimes fell short of what was desirable for this specialist work. We do not wish to imply criticism of voluntary bodies or local authorities in exercising their child care responsibilities. It seems to us that the shortage of specialist provision (in so far as there is one) is at least in part attributable to the present multiplicity of authorities, which may encourage each to make its own provision, resulting in a number of small "multi-purpose" establishments, from which specially difficult cases tend to be rejected as unsuitable and refractory, and may thus proceed to approved schools. A concentration of responsibility at education authority level, as we are recommending in a later chapter, would offer opportunities, in many areas, for a re-appraisal of the functions of a number of existing children's homes within each area, with greater opportunity for reorganisation and a greater degree of specialisation in each.

The Wider Problem

172. The problem confronting child care authorities in providing for children in their care suffering from maladjustment or mental handicap—as, for that matter, the problems arising where children similarly suffering are brought before the juvenile courts at present on the grounds of juvenile delinquency—cannot, it seems to us, be satisfactorily resolved unless seen in the wider context of the general educational provision for all such children, whatever the circumstances in which their needs first come to public notice.

173. For children of school-age the duty of ascertaining physical or mental handicap such as to require special educational treatment at present rests with education authorities, and the relevant regulations define the various categories as including (among others)—

(a) maladjusted pupils, that is to say, pupils who suffer from emotional instability or psychological disturbance; and

(b) mentally handicapped pupils, that is to say, pupils who have little natural ability.

174. While in the past, ascertainment of the number of such children in Scotland has been rendered difficult in the absence of clearly defined standards, we understand that two working parties, representative of educational and medical interests, have been set up by the Scottish Education Department to give guidance on ascertainment for both groups. The Working Party on standards of mental handicap has already reported,* and their Report has, we are informed, been sent to education authorities for their guidance. As a result, improvement in standards of ascertainment may be expected. The great majority of such children attend day special schools, and those of still lower ability receive training in occupational centres. Those who are completely unresponsive to education or training, or who exhibit serious behaviour problems, are referred to local health authorities and may be placed in mental hospitals.

175. While no doubt much remains to be done in that field, the evidence before us suggested that even more serious shortcomings were to be found in relation to provision for maladjusted children. Maladjustment is, of course, not an exact term and may vary in degree. In many cases the children may appropriately attend ordinary day schools, their teachers and parents receiving guidance and advice from the child guidance service of the education authority. In other cases severe maladjustment, particularly where coupled with adverse home circumstances, may make attendance at a residential school desirable, and here the evidence before us suggested that there was a serious shortage of provision. Such limited provision as exists is made, with a few notable exceptions, by voluntary agencies.

176. The evidence before us also suggested that there is at present a serious gap in existing arrangements for children suffering from serious maladjustment, especially where the child also suffers from mental handicap. In an appreciable number of cases, delinquency is simply a manifestation of maladjustment or emotional disturbance, often associated with impaired intelligence, and in these circumstances it is not surprising that difficulties as to placings should arise. On the one hand, there is for practical purposes no existing provision for such cases in the residential homes and schools already mentioned; on the hospital side, there are at present only three psychiatric in-patient children's units operating in Scotland. In other hospitals there are obvious difficulties in coping with more than a limited number of such cases in view of their effect on other less disturbed children. We understand that plans are in hand to provide additional hospital accommodation for children suffering from mental defect. We hope that these will be pressed ahead vigorously, and that they will take due account of the needs of such children who are also suffering from serious emotional disturbance.

177. Further, quite apart from the problems of defective or mentally handicapped children, a serious problem arises in junior secondary schools in the treatment of maladjusted children. Maladjustment, often arising from family and environmental factors, frequently reveals itself in an apparent failing away

---

* "Degrees of Mental Handicap": Report of the Working Party on Standards of Ascertainment for Scottish Schoolchildren, 1961.

of school attainment standards, apparent apathy and sometimes truancy; all of these are in turn not infrequently merely the incipient features of delinquency. Within the range of residential schools, there appears to us to be a real need for short-term establishments which would in that sense be "adjustment schools".

178.   The findings of the Working Party on Maladjustment may, we hope, be expected to induce a fresh impetus in this field, and may in due course lead to improved residential school provision. For our part, we can only say this. If, as we have indicated, the problem of juvenile delinquency can with greatest hope of success be treated on the basis of an educational and preventive principle, the importance of early ascertainment of impaired intelligence and maladjustment, and appropriate special educational provision to meet such needs, is plain. We do not suggest that more than a limited proportion of juvenile delinquency calls for treatment on that basis. Action in these directions would, we consider, nevertheless be likely to make an appreciable contribution to the problem, and would go far in many cases to prevent more serious delinquency in later years. Better provision in the directions suggested would also, in our view, help to solve many of the problems, to which we have referred, arising in the child care and approved school fields. Practically all the measures which we have mentioned entail increased educational provision of various kinds; as we have indicated, ascertainment is at present the responsibility of the education authorities. For that reason, as well as others which we discuss later, it seems to us that the problem of residential provision for all classes of children requiring special measures of education, care and training, can be assessed in proper balance and perspective only if handled by a single authority, namely, the education authority, to whom in consequence the present child care functions of local authorities should be transferred. Approved schools are already within the field of educational provision, and with such adjustments as we discuss below, would in future, under our recommendations, simply take their place as part of the total range of residential schools offering special educational provision.

APPROVED SCHOOLS—ANOTHER ASPECT OF THE WIDER PROBLEM

179.   Approved schools, unlike special schools or for that matter psychiatric hospitals, at present exist to meet the needs of children committed to their care by juvenile courts for educational and training measures. On this account they have no doubt tended to be singled out in the public mind as distinct, entirely separate, and in some sense punitive establishments, an impression possibly furthered by the separate arrangements which in nearly all cases govern their financing and administration. Such an impression, however, neither accords with the statutory position nor with the actual facts. The law already recognises approved schools as being basically special residential schools to which juvenile offenders and juveniles in need of "care or protection" alike may be committed. In actual fact, while the majority of children sent to approved schools do so following the commission of delinquent acts, a number are committed on "care or protection" proceedings (including proceedings for truancy). In the experience of those most closely concerned with these children, all, regardless of their present legal classification, are found to be in greater or lesser degree disturbed children. Further, implicit in an order for residential training of this kind is normally a need for sustained and more prolonged training process, both in terms of social training and formal educational instruction, such children in most cases being those whose history shows a fairly lengthy record of disturbed

family and environmental conditions. In many cases the children concerned (or their relatives) have already been at various times in the hands of social agencies of various kinds—to whose efforts they have for whatever reason failed to respond. Equally, in some cases children in approved schools appear to be there either because no more suitable forms of residential training exist, or because of the lack of adequate machinery for early detection of maladjustment and handicap. There is therefore the closest inter-relationship between approved schools and the other forms of residential training already discussed. Many of the difficulties facing approved schools are simply a reflection either of earlier difficulties which have remained unresolved, or of inadequacies of provision in other directions.

180.   There are at present twenty-four Scottish approved schools, twenty-two under voluntary management and two managed by Glasgow Education Authority. We understand that two additional schools, for boys in the $14\frac{1}{2}$ to 16 age range, are about to be opened under Church of Scotland and Roman Catholic auspices respectively. The approved schools are classified according to the sex, religion, and age of the pupils, and are further classified as junior, intermediate and senior schools for pupils of different ages.

181.   The evidence which we received suggested that while the great majority of committals were properly made, there is a minority, including those involving children suffering from serious maladjustment or mental handicap (to which we have already referred) almost all of whom might have been expected to be assigned to other forms of residential training had the necessary facilities been available. We were also told that it was not unknown for partially deaf or blind children, epileptics, physically handicapped delinquents and pregnant girls to be committed. The fact that such cases arise, even though the total may be numerically small and in some cases the degree of disability not such as to render the committals valueless, seems to us to illustrate the need for early diagnosis or ascertainment and for improved arrangements for assessment of juvenile offenders before any decision as to residential training of any kind is taken. The extended provision for special educational facilities for children suffering from various forms of handicap, which we have already urged, will, we hope, make approved school placings of this kind increasingly rare.

182.   Equally, a number of the children sent to approved schools at present are committed on ground of persistent truancy. The schools can, we think, help many of these children and we should not expect them in future to be wholly excluded. Nevertheless, in the light of our recommendation for the development of one or more short-term residential schools under education authority auspices designed to provide a short "adjustment" course of training primarily for pupils of junior secondary school age, some reduction of "truancy" committals to approved schools might be expected. If "adjustment" schools of the kind were in being, we would hope that most of the children sent there for special educational provision would be so sent at a stage sufficiently early to avoid any need for their appearance before the juvenile panels. Not every case could be detected at such a stage, however, and situations could still arise in which appearance before the panel resulted, and in which the child could equally benefit from more prolonged residential school training. We therefore intend that the panels' powers to order residential training should extend to any special residential school provided now or in future by education authorities or recognised voluntary agencies, including those at present classed as approved schools.

183. It was represented to us that the present approved school system in Scotland, even assuming that the various problems to which we have already referred were overcome, offered an insufficient variety of regime, and that in many schools the age-spread was much too wide. We accept that in view of the relatively small total number of schools in Scotland and given the present classification by age, sex, and religion, the scope for further specialisation must at any time be severely limited. We also appreciate that, within the existing framework, each school has to some extent its own distinctive characteristics and tradition built up over the years, and that even within the existing classifications there is a measure of diversity, the regime in some schools placing more emphasis on the disciplinary aspect than in others whose characteristics may be more nearly akin to that of a children's home. Provision has more recently been made for two special categories of boys—at Rossie Farm School and Loaningdale School, Biggar. Since early 1962 a section of Rossie Farm School has been used to deal with up to 25 boys of all denominations, age 13 and over, (already committed by the courts) who present persistent problems and are not amenable to the normal discipline of the other schools, or who are persistent absconders. The boys are subject to the normal school regime but the building is more secure, and constant supervision and close review are possible. Loaningdale School (opened in January 1963) is dealing with Protestant boys, age 13 and over, who are all reasonably intelligent and who seem likely to benefit from intensive social instruction, and may thus be expected to qualify more rapidly than is usual for return into the community. The arrangements at Loaningdale will no doubt be subject to further development in the light of experience.

184. We have already noted the very wide age-range which each of the existing approved schools has to cover. Ideally, it might be thought that the aim should be to secure a redistribution of functions within the existing schools so as to provide separately for three age groups—those under 11, those in the 11–14 age group and those of over 14. We accept that the wide variation in date of committal makes this impracticable, and that in many cases it would be very undesirable to transfer a child, committed at, say, the age of 13 to another school simply because he had attained the age of 14. Many approved school pupils come from a disturbed home environment and find in the schools for the first time a sense of security hitherto lacking in their lives. Changes of school within relatively short periods might well in many cases go far to undo the beneficial results already achieved. We do, however, consider that particularly within the larger schools there is scope for development of age-grouping by means of the "house" system. We realise that within the approved school system in more recent years there has been increasing emphasis on the provision of social as distinct from purely formal education, and that several schools are already providing "houses" and social work staff. We welcome this development, which we should like to see extended and accelerated.

185. The term "approved school" has in process of time come to have unfortunate connotations. Whatever term is used, the schools can never wholly avoid being singled out, at any rate by those closely connected with their clientele, as in some sense punitive establishments, and it would be unrealistic to assume that the stigma existing in the public mind will readily disappear. Nevertheless, under our proposals we think it appropriate that the term "approved school" should cease to be used for official purposes and that in so

far as a generic name is needed for the group, they should simply be described as "residential schools". Within the frame-work which we have described, the present approved schools would then become simply part of the range of residential schools catering for the wide variety of children whose needs, for whatever reason, cannot be adequately met within the normal educational provision, and all of whom can properly be said to be in need of special education and training of a kind which can be supplied only in a residential school.

DURATION OF RESIDENTIAL MEASURES AND CONTINUING SUPERVISION

186.   Under our proposals we contemplate that, in general, orders by the panels for placing in a residential school would be of indeterminate duration—the panel in each case directing a review after such period as it considered appropriate. Under these arrangements, the present legal powers of the school managers acting *in loco parentis* would be abolished. Children in such schools would remain within the jurisdiction of the panels, the managers acting in practice as temporary "foster parents" to the same extent as children's homes at present in the case of children placed there by a local authority. The schools would then be responsible as at present for all day-to-day matters of care and training, subject to the general oversight of the panel (through the director of social education). The termination of residential training would be by order of the panel, and would in practice arise on a recommendation by the managers and the director of social education, who would already be familiar with the child's history and background; and who up to that point would have been maintaining contact with the child and his family throughout, and would in many cases have been engaged in casework in the home during the period of the child's removal. Return to the community would be coupled with a period of supervision by a social worker of the social education department, again subject to the panel's directions. "After-care" as such would disappear. The situation would simply be that a period of more intensive residential training was followed by a period of care, supervision and guidance on return to community life. Occasions might arise where there could be a conflict of view on the question of a child's return home as between the social education department (in the light of their knowledge of the home) and the managers (in the light of the child's progress in school). Such disputes would normally be resolved in discussion between the two, but exceptionally in face of disagreement the matter would fall to be resolved by the panel.

GENERAL OBSERVATIONS ON RESIDENTIAL FACILITIES

187.   The evidence before us has led us to the conclusion that the need for residential training facilities can be met only by a comprehensive approach by a single agency exercising statutory responsibility both for children's homes and residential schools of all kinds provided within the public field. On the one hand there is an urgent need for the provision of special educational facilities (residential and non-residential) for those suffering from mental and physical handicap or from maladjustment, factors which equally present serious problems at present in children's homes. Within the wider unified organisation which we are recommending, it may in some cases be possible, as a contribution towards the necessary facilities, to introduce a greater degree of specialisation in certain existing children's homes. Additional residential provision will,

however, undoubtedly be required and should, we consider, be provided by education authorities under their existing powers, either singly or in combination on a regional basis. Such provision should, for the reasons discussed in paragraphs 177 and 182, include in particular facilities for short-term residential education for pupils of junior secondary school age.

188.   The evidence also suggested that there is a need for separate residential school provision for younger boys (i.e., under the age of 11). The number of approved school pupils presently within this age-group would in itself seem to support this view. It might well be found, assuming the various other types of provision which we have already recommended are developed by education authorities, that the needs of this age-group are already substantially met within that provision. In so far as special provision for this age-group is at present or may continue in future to be needed, the matter seems to us in any event to be one for appropriate education authority provision, rather than by provision of any new and separate residential school within the present approved school framework.

189.   In all these fields voluntary agencies have hitherto played a vital part and, as we have indicated in paragraph 175, they are at the present time virtually the sole providers of residential schools for maladjusted children. We would by no means wish to see any reduction in voluntary effort in this sphere. The lack of provision is, however, such that the major part must clearly fall to education authorities.

190.   We received little criticism of the present arrangements governing the schools' management, which (apart from the two Glasgow schools) rests with committees of voluntary managers. We do not suggest any basic change in these arrangements. We have, of course, already indicated (paragraph 186) that our proposals imply an alteration in the legal responsibility for children committed to them for residential training by the juvenile panels, continuing oversight in these cases to be vested in the panels and to be exercised through the social education department.

JUNIOR DETENTION CENTRES

191.   Our proposals envisage development of a wide range of special residential provision by education authorities, including shorter-term residential schools for boys of 13 to under 16. The age range covered is broadly the same as that for which junior detention centres have sometimes been proposed. No junior detention centre has yet been set up in Scotland, but in our view both types of institution, the shorter-term school and the junior detention centre, are intended to cater for the needs of broadly the same type of pupil, namely, the boy of average intelligence whose record does not show signs of deep-seated criminality or disturbance, and who is likely to respond to a fairly limited period of sustained education and training within a disciplined environment. In our view, juvenile offenders of this age-group in Scotland could within the general framework of our recommendations more appropriately be dealt within the short-term residential school provision of the kind which we have already discussed. In that event we do not consider that there would be any need to institute junior detention centres. The form of training appropriate for boys of this age range (13 to under 16) can, we think, best be carried out within the

discipline of a residential school, and under our proposals we consider it appropriate that such schools should be administered within the general educational system and not as part of the State penal system, which we assume would be the case were a junior detention centre to be introduced.

OTHER SHORT-TERM DETENTION

192.   We discuss existing remand home facilities in a later Chapter, but it is appropriate at this stage, in considering the range of powers of the juvenile panels, to indicate that our proposals imply the abolition of detention in a remand home as a method of treatment. In reaching this conclusion we have taken account of the views of experienced witnesses, the general tenor of which was to cast serious doubt on the efficacy of this form of detention as a method of treatment. Remand home detention, which may at present be applied to juvenile offenders under the age of 14 for periods of up to 28 days, seems to us to be essentially a punitive form of treatment, the punishment being by deprivation of liberty. Under present circumstances, juvenile courts may also order remand home detention for juvenile offenders between the ages of 14 and 17. As we have already indicated, in so far as there is a need for shorter-term residential training for this older age-group, we consider that it can be more effectively met by committal to a short-term residential school of the kind which we have recommended. As regards the younger age-group, in our view where residential treatment is really required for younger children, i.e., those under 14, to be effective it requires a period of several months, not weeks. The general view which emerged in the discussions before us was that remand home detention as at present understood appeared to be almost always ineffective, and that, so far as younger children were concerned, the idea of punitive detention, even if "scaled down" to 28 days or less, had little to commend it. We do not contemplate that by any means all of the children at present ordered to undergo remand home detention would in future require residential training for a lengthy period, and many of these children may not, we think, need residential training at all. In so far as the underlying purpose of such committals is at present that of punishment by deprivation, such cases could more appropriately in our view be dealt with by other non-residential measures within the range of powers which we are recommending for the juvenile panels.

193.   Even if it were considered that the idea of punitive detention by removal of younger children from home for relatively short periods might exceptionally be justified, it has, we think, to be recognised that the provision of such facilities would create serious practical problems. Remand home detention as at present operated takes place in premises whose primary function is that of safe keeping and assessment of the needs of children held there pending decision as to the treatment measures to be applied. Such facilities as at present exist have, with certain exceptions, hitherto been quite inadequate, and the homes' function as assessment centres seems to us to be quite incompatible with the entirely different role of places of detention as a punitive measure. It is essential to our proposals that the first of these functions should be given full and proper recognition, and in such circumstances it is clear that if the idea of punitive detention for younger children were retained, entirely separate provision for this form of treatment would have to be made. On the information before us, the total number of younger children in Scotland for whom on any reasonable criterion such provision could ever be likely to be regarded as appropriate would, we

77

consider, be such as to justify only one such establishment. While it is possible under present arrangements to commit children for punitive detention in remand home premises (however unsuitable they may be) within relatively easy access to their own homes, this would be impracticable in future. For our part we could not contemplate the alternative, which is that children under 14 would in future be accommodated in a single national detention home—of necessity in many cases far removed from the inmates' home areas. Accordingly, in the light both of the general considerations as well as the practical difficulties already mentioned, we recommend that remand home detention as a method of treatment should be abolished.

Compulsory Measures
Under The Mental Health (Scotland) Act, 1960

194.   Under present provisions the compulsory hospital detention (or reception into guardianship under the local health authority) of persons suffering from serious mental disorder is carried out under statutory procedures involving a Sheriff's order under Part IV of the Mental Health (Scotland) Act, 1960. Separate procedure is provided under Part V of the Act for action in relation to such persons subject to criminal proceedings in the Sheriff Court or in the High Court of Justiciary. At present the juvenile courts have no power to make such orders and, where it appears to them that any child brought before them (whether in criminal or "care or protection" proceedings) may be suffering from mental disorder, the case must be remitted to the Sheriff Court.

195.   The principle of compulsory measures by reason of mental disorder being subject to judicial order is of long standing, and is of course essentially intended as a safeguard for the liberty of the subject. In present-day conditions, situations in which compulsory measures of the kind are likely to be essential in the case of children under 16 are likely to be comparatively few. In any event, since the question depends essentially on medical evidence on standards laid down by law, we consider it inappropriate that the juvenile panels should be empowered to make such orders. If they were so empowered, their orders would in any event require to be subject to a right of appeal to the Sheriff, and it seems appropriate that all compulsory measures in this field should continue to be authorised by the Sheriff. Under our proposals, where any question of the kind arises, it would be for the reporter to the panel to decide whether or not to refer the case to the appropriate medical authorities with a view to action under Part IV of the Act. The great majority of cases would, we contemplate, be dealt with in this way without referral to the panel. Exceptionally, there would continue to be a few cases in which it was considered appropriate, both in the interests of the child's treatment and for the protection of others, that he should be made subject to hospital measures involving special security. Such cases would be few among juvenile offenders under the age of 16, and would be most likely to arise in situations involving homicidal acts or acts of serious physical violence. Under our proposals we consider that such cases would continue to be dealt with under the procedure provided for in Part V of the 1960 Act in that they would be referred by the reporter at the outset to the procurator fiscal. In cases falling short of that, the choice of procedure, where this was in any way in doubt, would be a matter for arrangement between the reporter to the panel and the procurator fiscal.

196. It may be convenient at this stage to summarise our recommendations as to the powers of the juvenile panels as discussed earlier in this Chapter, as extending to the following:

(1) decision to take no action;
(2) admonition (with or without a supervision order);
(3) attendance centre training;
(4) finding of caution on the parents (normally with a supervision order on the child);
(5) assumption of supervisory jurisdiction over the child—
    (*a*) the child living at home; or
    (*b*) where the situation so requires, including the additional requirement that he should be received into public care (under the day-to-day charge of a public or recognised voluntary agency); and thus including where necessary residence in a children's home or residential school.

"Residential school" in this context should be taken to include all schools within the existing approved school system and every residential school offering special educational facilities provided by an education authority or a recognised voluntary body. The foregoing relates to the powers which we recommend should be conferred on the juvenile panels by statute, and has to be read in the light of our comments as to the variety of other steps which might well be taken by the panels in agreement with the parents, with or without a formal order by the panels.

CHAPTER IX

Duration of Orders by the Panels, Rights of Appeal and Enforcement

DURATION OF ORDERS

197. We have already recommended that all orders by the juvenile panels should be open to appeal to the Sheriff within a specified period from the date on which they are made. We have also recommended that a child, once subject to the panel's jurisdiction, should in principle remain thereunder for such a period as the panel may consider necessary in the light of the child's training needs. Indeed, we consider it essential, if those needs are to be adequately met, that the panel should not be hampered by rigid statutory formulae governing the duration of particular forms of training. No doubt in practice and having regard to practical questions of administration, many of the panel's orders will from the outset stipulate a specific period of training—towards the end of which the child's progress will on their direction automatically come under their review. At that stage, in the light of circumstances, the case may be discharged, the existing order continued for a further period, or an entirely fresh type of order made. Equally, in our view, it should be open to the director of the social education department at any stage to bring a case before the panel for further review if it appears to him that the measures already ordered by the panel were not proving

efficacious and should be reconsidered; or, if they had proved to be effective, to recommend their termination. Accordingly, in addition to the initial right of appeal against an order when made, we recommend that any subsequent order by the panel involving a greater measure of deprivation of parental rights, e.g., by subsequently adding to a supervision order a requirement that the child should be received into public care or by substituting for the latter requirement an order for admission to a residential school, would similarly be subject to right of appeal. Further, since orders would frequently be of indeterminate duration, we consider that there should be a statutory right of appeal to the Sheriff in every case against the continuance of an order at annual intervals. Within these general limits, transfer on the panel's order between, e.g., one children's home and another, or between one residential school and another, would not be subject to appeal.

198.　The jurisdiction of the juvenile panels should in our view terminate in any event on the child's attaining the age of 16. Cases could then arise where a child is placed under supervision or ordered residential treatment at a relatively late age—it being clear that the training ought to be continued beyond the age of 16. In these circumstances we consider that the panels should automatically review such cases immediately before attainment of that age-limit, but that they should have power to continue measures, where considered appropriate, for further periods (subject to the rights of appeal already discussed) up to the age of 18. On attainment of that age their powers of supervision in any form would automatically cease. The panel's jurisdiction beyond the age of 16 would extend only to children already under their supervision prior to that age. First referrals would, as we have indicated, arise only in relation to children under 16.

ENFORCEMENT OF DECISIONS BY THE JUVENILE PANEL

199.　Under our recommendations, orders made by the juvenile panels would have full force in law from the date on which they were made, subject to the right of appeal to the Sheriff already discussed. In normal circumstances difficulties of enforcement are unlikely, we think, to arise in securing the attendance of children and parents. Where for any reason, however, it is necessary to invoke the sanctions of the law to secure attendance, we contemplate that this would be done by the reporter on a summary form of application to the Sheriff Summary Court, which could then ordain the parties concerned to appear before the panel, or in appropriate cases grant warrant of apprehension. Failure to appear on citation would attract the normal sanctions of the law before the criminal courts.

200.　While in general we do not envisage that difficulties will frequently occur as to enforcement of the panel's decisions, we think that such situations might on occasion arise on such matters as finding of caution. Cases may conceivably arise where a parent, having agreed before the panel to find caution, subsequently makes no attempt to do so simply out of carelessness or spleen, although on all the evidence he could without tremendous effort or sacrifice reasonably be expected to find the money. Finding of caution would be subject to the general right of appeal to the Sheriff at the time it was ordered. If thereafter caution is not lodged it should be open to the reporter to the panel to apply to the Sheriff to ordain caution judicially; any question of enforcement thereafter would he governed by the procedure for caution ordained by a criminal court. Equally, there may exceptionally be situations where on a parent's first or subsequent appearance before the panel, his whole attitude and demeanour is so unreasonable and insolent as to amount to what would in a court of law be contempt. We recommend that after a finding to this effect by the Sheriff on a statement of facts by the panel, the Sheriff should be empowered to deal with the matter by fine or imprisonment.

201. We have already indicated the objections to any idea of placing parents themselves directly under supervision. For similar reasons we have rejected suggestions for additional sanctions against parents in circumstances in which they appeared to be uncooperative in their relations with officers supervising their children under panel orders. Situations of this kind no doubt from time to time arise, in which the parents, having agreed to the making of a supervision order and to co-operate fully with the supervising officer, subsequently refuse to co-operate. This is not, of course, a new situation and is no doubt familiar to probation officers and others. Essentially, supervision of the kind starts from the assumption of willingness to co-operate, and over a very wide field it must, we think, be left to the essential skills of the case-worker to overcome initial difficulties of the kind. Faced with such attitudes, there appear at present to be two ultimate sanctions—that the parents' conduct eventually becomes so serious as to justify criminal proceedings for neglect, or that the situation develops to an extent which offers grounds justifying a further order for the child's removal from home. The whole purpose of supervision must, of course, be to prevent either of these situations arising—though it would be unrealistic to assume that even under the new arrangements recommended this could never arise. The possibility that the panel might order the child's removal from home would remain in the background, though it is assumed that in such circumstances the panel would issue a series of stern warnings before deciding on more drastic action.

202. Cases will undoubtedly arise in which inadequate, aggressive and argumentative parents are initially prepared to agree before the panel that their children should be subject to a supervision order, simply as a means of disposing of the matter and with no intention of co-operating subsequently. All this may well arise against a background of fairly minor misbehaviour arising from a lack of parental guidance and where on any reasonable criterion there could be no immediate question of removing the child from the home. The child himself may be amenable to supervision, but for the parental obstruction. In these circumstances it was suggested to us that there might possibly be an argument for making such conduct (if amounting to repeated, wilful and unreasonable refusal to co-operate after successive warnings by the panel) an offence punishable in the Sheriff Court by fine or imprisonment.

203. On the general arguments already outlined as to the nature of supervision (which is essentially family case-work) it seems to us very doubtful whether such measures would be appropriate. Practical questions would be bound to arise as to whether the parents' conduct could really be said to amount to repeated, wilful and unreasonable refusal to co-operate. At present in such circumstances parental behaviour of the kind is not a criminal offence, and it would seem rather paradoxical if the creation of juvenile panels, designed to assist and further parental responsibility within the family context, were to result in the creation of new classes of criminal offence falling considerably

short of those already recognised in this sphere. The system of juvenile panels as a whole presupposes the need to deal at the earliest possible stage with neglect, actual or incipient, and is in fact based on a recognition that parental failure can extend to a far wider variety of situations than the criminal law at present recognises as neglect. It would, however, seem indefensible to us that, at the very time when preventive and remedial action is being instituted, in the shape of supervision by a social worker, conduct of this kind (falling far short of cruelty or neglect in any presently recognised legal sense) should be liable within a short space to be cited as a criminal offence.

CONTINUATION FOR INQUIRY AND ASSESSMENT

204. It is implicit in our proposals that the juvenile panels should have power to continue cases for inquiries for periods which we suggest should, subject to a power of renewal, be subject to a maximum of 21 days.

INTERIM CUSTODY PENDING APPEARANCE BEFORE THE PANELS

205. Our attention was drawn to Section 71 of the 1937 Act, which empowers juvenile courts to make interim orders for further inquiries in the case of children and young persons who have been detained in a place of safety by the police or other authorised persons pending appearance before the courts. Sub-section (1) empowers the police or the other persons mentioned to take such action in the child's interests until he can be brought before a juvenile court on "care or protection" proceedings. It was suggested to us that unnecessary delays sometimes occur in bringing such cases before the courts, partly because the sub-section does not place a clear duty on any specific agency to do so, and partly because the provision has been interpreted (in our view erroneously) in some areas as implying authority to retain the child in custody without further warrant for a period of up to 28 days. In our view the 28 day maximum relates only to the powers of juvenile courts under sub-section (2) and not to a warrant for interim detention obtained under sub-section (1). In the latter case the general rule under the Summary Jurisdiction (Scotland) Act, 1954 (which by virtue of Section 52(2) of the 1937 Act applies to juvenile court procedure generally), is operative, namely, that on being taken into custody a juvenile should be produced wherever possible on the first lawful day. If, however, the question is in any way in doubt, we consider that it ought to be the subject of specific provision in legislation governing the bringing of children before the juvenile panels. In all cases, irrespective of the circumstances in which particular cases come to light, the general rule should operate, namely, that the child is, wherever practicable, to be brought before a juvenile panel on the first lawful day following his retention in custody.

CHAPTER X

Facilities for Assessment

206. All our proposals throughout presuppose that adequate facilities for assessment exist. If indeed the juvenile panels are to provide a more discriminating machinery for intervention and the application of appropriate measures of education and training, the existence of such facilities is basic to our proposals. We should make it clear at the outset that we attach great importance to the availability of such facilities in the community, so that only in exceptional circumstances will it be necessary for the child to be separated from his parents pending a decision on treatment measures. The task of making these assessments will fall on the social education department, using where necessary the psychiatric services of the National Hospital Service. However, it must be accepted that circumstances will arise in which the child cannot be left with his parents and must stay during this period in a residential establishment.

PRESENT ARRANGEMENTS

207. Where juveniles who appear before the courts at present are remanded in custody, they are almost always remanded to a remand home. Juveniles aged 17–21, at any rate from Glasgow and the South-West, are now in these circumstances being sent to Polmont or Longriggend remand units, and the unit also receives a number of younger juveniles certified by the courts as too unruly or depraved for remand to a remand home.

208. In earlier times children were simply remanded in police custody, and remand homes as first conceived were no doubt seen as an improvement on this, exercising in a scaled-down manner the three functions performed by prisons in relation to adults, namely, safe custody pending appearance, detention as a punishment, and latterly places of safe custody for inquiries regarding disposal, as well as providing interim places of safety for children in moral or physical danger. We have already recommended (paragraph 193) that remand home detention as a method of punishment should be abolished.

209. Remand homes were recently reviewed by the Ellis Committee (a special Committee of the Scottish Advisory Council on Child Care).* That Committee were asked to consider "the principles on which remand homes should be provided and operated in future", though in view of our own remit they were debarred from considering the law relating to the courts' use of remand homes. In short, they had to assume that remand homes might have to continue to exercise all their present functions, and on that basis the principles on which they should be run. The Committee found that existing remand homes, with certain notable exceptions, fell far short in terms of accommodation, staff and diagnostic facilities, of what was desirable and necessary—in some cases deplorably so. Their main recommendations were that—

(1) children 8–11 should wherever practicable be remanded to children's homes under the Children Act, 1948;

(2) girls of 12 and over should be admitted to a central remand home for girls, and boys and girls should no longer be accommodated in mixed homes;

---

* "Remand Homes": Report of a Special Committee of the Scottish Advisory Council on Child Care: Cmnd. 1588: 1961.

83

(3) full diagnostic facilities should be available for each home; and salaries, conditions of service and training of remand home staff should be negotiated on a national basis;

(4) responsibility for remand homes should be transferred to the Secretary of State;

(5) in remoter areas places of temporary custody of the existing type should be continued—strictly for overnight stay *en route* to a regional remand home.

210. In a circular to local authorities issued in December, 1962, the Scottish Education Department indicated that the Secretary of State in effect accepted the Committee's strictures on the majority of existing remand homes. The publication of the Report had itself been followed by proposals from several local authorities. The Secretary of State also indicated that in his view—a view which we beg to endorse—the remand homes service is best regarded as a part of the wider child care service and can more appropriately be developed in association with that service rather than as a separate small organisation; and he had therefore decided that responsibility for remand homes should, for the present at least, remain with local authorities. As to salaries, staff and training, he was entering into discussion with the local authority associations. As to remand accommodation for girls over 12, the remand home for girls in Glasgow already catered, by arrangement with other local authorities, for over half the girls in Scotland placed in remand homes and these arrangements could be further extended. In his view, however, Glasgow could not be expected to cater for the whole of Scotland, and in some areas mixed homes would probably continue to be necessary. As to remand of all children under 12 to Children Act homes or reception centres, a decision was deferred pending our own deliberations. (It is understood that amending legislation would be necessary for such a step in any event.) Finally, the Secretary of State called on all authorities to give urgent consideration to remand provision in or for their areas, and to inform him of the arrangements they proposed for the future.

FUTURE PATTERN

211. There seems, accordingly, to be prospect that within a reasonable period proposals will emerge which will provide at least the nucleus of facilities which could reasonably be developed so as to operate as regional remand homes for Glasgow and the South-West; Edinburgh, parts of Fife and the Borders; Dundee—no doubt covering parts of Fife, Angus and Perthshire; and Aberdeen. The extreme northern counties present a special problem.

212. Under our own proposals, it would appear to be desirable that assessment centres should be operated as an integral part of the social education service. It would no doubt be necessary to rely heavily for specialist assistance both from the educational child guidance service and the school medical service (all of which would incidentally form part of the comprehensive social education department which we are recommending, operated within the education service as a whole), and from the psychiatric service of the National Hospital Service. They should in our view be available for assessment purposes of any child in need, whether or not his circumstances are such as to justify a referral to the juvenile panels; and their use as reporting centres on an "out-client" basis (as well as offering accommodation for children who require in their own interests to be removed from home for assessment purposes) should be encouraged.

213.   However well facilities for assessment in the community are developed, there will remain a need for accommodation of some kind for safe custody of children in certain circumstances pending appearance before the juvenile panels. Under our proposals the argument that "delinquents" should never be housed even temporarily in children's homes will in some measure disappear, and we agree with the Ellis Committee that younger children under 12 could well be accommodated both in these circumstances and on remand for assessment in such homes and centres. This presupposes a corresponding development in making diagnostic and assessment facilities available for such establishments. We also consider that there should be flexible arrangements for children under 12, the juvenile panels being empowered, for special reasons, in particular cases to direct remand to one of the assessment centres maintained primarily for the older age-group.

214.   For children of 12 and under 16, we contemplate that regional residential assessment centres would also serve as places of safe custody pending first appearance. Such centres would, it is assumed, be secure establishments; otherwise there is risk of continuance of present practice in at least one area whereby older children under 16, being found to be unsuitable for the local remand home (designed primarily for younger children) are sometimes certified by the courts as unruly and remanded to prison (and thus proceeding to the Longriggend or Polmont units for 17–21s).

215.   If, as we suggest, there should for older children be broadly four main regional assessment centres based on the four cities, with assessments arrived at on a "team" basis, it should be quite possible for the staffs of the social education services principally concerned to familiarise themselves at first hand with the range of homes and schools available throughout Scotland, and recommendations for placings to be made accordingly to the juvenile panels. We recommend that, as part of the assessment facilities available to him, the director of social education should have a definite and recognised claim on part of the time of the local hospital psychiatric services, and it would be for the latter to organise their arrangements accordingly.

216.   Under our proposals, the assessment centres, and for younger children, children's homes, would continue to act as places of safe custody pending appearance before the panels. In the more remote areas, simple overnight accommodation would continue to be needed pending conveyance to the nearest assessment centre. The name "remand home" would disappear and the centres should be described as "residential assessment centres", which would in fact be no more than a true reflection of their essential purpose. One consequence of our proposals would be that the present arrangements whereby places in approved schools are allocated by the Scottish Education Department in response to individual requests, usually made by probation officers and education authorities, would be terminated. Arrangements would instead need to be made for lists of vacancies to be maintained at each of the main regional assessment centres, but this should not present any great difficulty.

217.   Remand or assessment centres are ultimately holding centres. However well-qualified the resident staff, there will always be limits to the contribution that they themselves can be expected to make; and in that sense such establishments are primarily a convenient means of holding the child in a stable environment, into which a variety of specialist advisers and consultants may enter for the purpose of diagnosis and assessment. It was suggested to us in the evidence which we received that, at present, remand in custody tends to be adopted almost automatically in many cases where residential measures are under consideration. While this is no doubt sometimes done for the convenience of visiting specialists, it has to be recognised that as a result in practice children are sometimes being held for periods of as much as 14 days, in the course of which they may be seen by a psychiatric consultant on only one occasion, possibly for an hour or less. In the light of the arrangements discussed in the previous paragraphs, we consider that the use of reporting, either to hospital clinics or to the assessment centres on an out-client basis, should be encouraged. We realise, however, that in many populous areas arrangements of this kind would be likely to face serious practical difficulties, in that the people likely to be affected will often tend to be those who have no knowledge and possibly some distrust of clinics, and to whom ideas of attending for set appointments are altogether foreign. On the other hand, we understand that in some areas, where no local remand home accommodation at present exists, arrangements are not infrequently made whereby a probation officer collects the child on the appropriate day for appointment with a specialist in the nearest larger centre. While it is clearly impracticable to lay down any rigid rule, we recommend that wherever residential measures are under consideration, the juvenile panels ought to consider carefully in every case whether, for the purposes of assessment, retention in custody is in fact essential; and we think that there may well be room for greater experiment in the use of reporting on an out-client basis to the appropriate centres or clinics.

POLICE POWERS OF REMAND IN CUSTODY

218.   Where the police apprehend a juvenile, they are empowered, under section 40 of the 1937 Act, to release him pending court appearance in certain circumstances. So far as common law offences are concerned, the power to release is understood to apply only to cases within the jurisdiction of the lower courts of summary jurisdiction and not to cases reserved to the Sheriff Court (in that bail in the latter cases is a matter for the procurator fiscal). One result at present is that, in at least one area, "sheriff court cases" are automatically retained in custody, pending first appearance. For under-16s, the arbitrary distinction between cases involving various types of common law offences appropriate for the Sheriff Court and the lower courts respectively, would, of course, disappear under our proposals, in that virtually all cases would come before the juvenile panels. The statutory provisions governing police discretion to liberate pending appearance would require to be re-framed accordingly.

219.   The general assumption underlying the present provision, which seems to us to be essentially sound, is that children will normally be liberated on an undertaking by the child or his parent for attendance in court, or on bail being found. The police, i.e., the officer in charge of the police station, is required to liberate unless—

(*a*) the charge is one of homicide or other grave crime;

(*b*) it is necessary to remove the child from association with any reputed criminal or prostitute;

(*c*) the officer has reason to believe that the child's liberation would defeat the ends of justice.

220.   If not liberated, the juvenile must be sent to a remand home pending first appearance (i.e., wherever possible, on the first lawful day): he can be retained in police custody only if the police officer certifies—

(*a*) that it is impracticable to send him to a remand home;

(*b*) that he is of so unruly a character that he cannot safely be detained there; or

(*c*) that by reason of state of health or mental or bodily condition it is inadvisable so to detain him.

In such cases the certificate has to be produced to the court.

221.   As to liberation or retention in custody, the provisions in paragraph 219 mean that in practice the police (and the officer in charge may in some cases be a sergeant) have a wide discretion. Items (*a*) and (*b*) would probably not cause serious dispute, but item (*c*) offers a very wide discretion. Again, as to overnight retention in police custody as opposed to custody in a remand home (paragraph 220), a wide discretion is conferred.

222.   While particular cases arising from time to time may be the subject of criticism, we found no firm evidence of serious over-use of the provisions, and equally it seems clear that the police will always require to have a wide measure of discretion, given the wide variety of circumstances in which they are called upon to act at any hour. There is, for example, little evidence of juveniles being unreasonably detained in police cells on the pretext of being too unruly for a remand home, and in so far as the problem does arise, it is probably confined to areas where the available remand accommodation is for practical purposes designed solely for younger children. In such a situation, the courts for their part may equally   as we have noted in paragraph 214—feel constrained, on the child's appearance before them, to order remand to the Longriggend or Polmont remand units. In such areas it seems to us that these difficulties could be largely resolved by entering into arrangements with neighbouring authorities which do have appropriate facilities for older children. The development of regional assessment centres on the lines we have recommended would in any event go far to remove such difficulties in future.

CHAPTER XI

Consequential Matters

223.   The general arrangements which we propose necessarily involve legislation which would, we contemplate, embody the main principles underlying our proposals, and would also include powers enabling rules to be made governing many of the detailed matters relating to the constitution of the

juvenile panels and the necessary procedural machinery. We have not sought to discuss all those matters in detail; many of them would, if our main proposals are accepted, no doubt be the subject of detailed examination by expert working parties. Having set out our broad intentions, we do not envisage that any of the procedural questions arising are by any means likely to be incapable of solution. We think it desirable, however, to comment on several consequential matters arising from our proposals.

OFFENCES INVOLVING CHILDREN AND ADULTS

224. Section 50 of the 1937 Act excludes from the jurisdiction of the juvenile courts cases in which a charge is made jointly against a child or young person and a person over the age of 17. This general provision does not, however, apply where a child or young person is charged with an offence, and a person over 17 is charged with aiding and abetting him. Under existing arrangements, juveniles and adults are not infrequently dealt with separately. While the matter cannot in our view be made the subject of invariable rule, we should expect under our proposals that the great majority of juveniles so involved would be referred at the outset to the juvenile panels. Even where, by virtue of the continuing Crown discretion, they were not, we recommend that in every case where a juvenile is exceptionally brought before a criminal court and is found to have committed an offence, that court should be empowered to remit the case to the appropriate juvenile panel for consideration of treatment measures.

FULL-TIME CHAIRMEN OF JUVENILE PANELS

225. In most areas we contemplate that appointments would be on a voluntary and part-time basis. In the largest urban areas, it might, we think, well be found necessary for the efficient working of individual panels and in view of the likely volume of business and frequency of sittings, to make provision for appointment of one or more full-time salaried chairmen of the panels. Such appointments would as in other cases be made by the Sheriff; provision should be made for salaries and conditions of appointment in these cases to be regulated under rules to be made by the Secretary of State.

PLACES OF SITTING AND HOURS

226. We consider that at present in many cases juvenile courts are being held in premises totally unsuited for the purpose. What is essentially required for the juvenile panels recommended under our proposals is relatively simple accommodation of the committee-room type, preferably in reasonably modern buildings, the room itself combining an atmosphere of simplicity and unobtrusive and unostentatious dignity. Sufficient waiting-rooms should be available. Sittings of the panels should be held in premises quite apart and dissociated entirely from the criminal courts and police stations. In many areas, suitable accommodation might well be found in schools (outwith school hours), public libraries and other public buildings. Hours of sittings must be a matter for local arrangement, but despite the difficulties of staffing and administration, we hope that it may be possible—bearing in mind the desirability of securing both parents' attendance—to arrange more widely for evening sittings and in some cases for Saturday sittings.

227. In some cases the panel's consideration of individual cases may well extend over a series of sittings at which, if the beneficial results we look to are to be achieved, the parents' continued attendance will be necessary. We consider that, if the co-operation of the parents is to be effectively enlisted in this way, arrangements should be made, where tile panel so approve, for reimbursement of expenses and possibly loss of earnings. We contemplate that there would have to be a minimum rate of outlay before expenses were reclaimable, and payment would be restricted to those on National Assistance or who could otherwise show serious need.

Research and Training

228. There was widespread agreement among the witnesses who appeared before us as to the need for further research both into factors governing child development and into the efficacy of particular forms of treatment for children in special need. We endorse this view. We commend the pioneer work already being done in these directions by Government-assisted research, and we hope that the universities themselves will be able to give an increasing measure of priority to this important work.

229. It is equally important that the results of such studies should be made fully available to those serving on the juvenile panels which we have recommended. We recommend that regular arrangements should be instituted in each area, as well as for periodic conferences at national level, to provide both basic information and wider interchange of ideas and experience among members of the panels. Indeed, such arrangements seem to us to be essential if the panels are to operate on an adequately informed basis, and a willingness to consider new ideas and methods is equally important to their essential flexibility of approach. Regular arrangements should in our view be made in each area for courses of lectures and discussions for all new members of panels (as well as refresher courses for serving members), extending both to the powers and machinery at their disposal, and including talks by members of the social education department and other local social services, as well as for visits to assessment centres, children's homes and residential schools.

Financial Arrangements for the Juvenile Panels

230. We recommend that the costs of accommodation and administration of the juvenile panels, including those of the reporter to the panel and his staff, should be met by the education authority. Provision should be made by rules (to be made by the Secretary of State) for reimbursement of travelling and subsistence expenses of members of the panels.

Police in Uniform

231. We understand that in some areas the view has been taken that the police should not, in appealing in connection with juvenile cases, be in uniform. We can see no sound basis for this, and recommend that in so far as such practices have developed they should be terminated.

Part Three

CHAPTER XII

The Matching Field organisation

232. Throughout our discussion of the operation of the juvenile panels, we have touched at various points on the need for a matching field organisation. The latter is, in our view, an essential counterpart to our proposals for the institution of the panels, and is indeed inseparable from them. While referral to the panel will be at the hand of the reporter to the panel, the reports reaching him and leading to such action may emanate from a wide variety of public and voluntary agencies, including the police. Moreover, in any given case one or other of these agencies may have an important role to play not merely in the detection of the individual child in need, but equally in the separate and subsequent stages involving assessment of those needs and the measures to be applied as a result.

THE PRINCIPLES GOVERNING THE NEW ORGANISATION

233. If it is to be effective, the system of juvenile panels presupposes in each area a central source of referrals through the panel's reporter, backed equally by simultaneous arrangements for informed and skilled advice channelled through a central agency, namely, the director of social education and his staff. The test in every case being the child's need for special educational measures, what is required is not some entirely new and different form of machinery for identification, diagnosis and assessment, and supervision; but a merging and reorganisation of those existing services whose primary concern is with the problems of the children in special need. The need for a greater measure of co-ordination of the local authority and voluntary services in this sphere has already been recognised in the Children and Young Persons Act, 1963, in that local authorities have been given new powers to try to prevent or as far as practicable remove, by informal action resting ultimately on the co-operation and consent of those concerned, the conditions which result in children coming into public care, whether by informal or compulsory procedures. Much has, of course, already been achieved in this sphere, and we have no doubt that it will be given added impetus as a result of the new statutory powers now conferred. It would, however, be entirely unrealistic to imagine that as a result situations calling for public intervention in the shape of compulsory measures will ever wholly disappear. Even with the improvements which may reasonably be expected as a result of the 1963 Act, some cases will continue undetected; in others which are detected, informal action will for various reasons prove ineffectual; and in some almost from the outset it will be clear to those concerned that it will be necessary to invoke the authority of the juvenile panels for the application of compulsory measures.

234. It will, we think, be evident from our earlier discussion of the juvenile panels that their work, while resting ultimately on their powers (as the duly constituted public authority in this field) to apply compulsory measures, is essentially an extension of that of the various existing local social services

concerned with children's needs. In many cases, the child will be brought before the panel where efforts by one or other of these agencies on a voluntary and persuasive basis have failed; or in circumstances in which the family (or members of it) are in one way or another already known to such services, even though the child himself may not hitherto have shown signs of serious disturbance. Indeed, as we have already indicated, it may well sometimes prove possible by bringing a child and his parents before the panel to secure their subsequent co-operation without the necessity of applying formal compulsory measures. In that way the panels may, we consider, be able in the course of full and frank discussion to lend the weight of their underlying authority—without resort to compulsion—in support of the efforts of the social workers concerned, in what is in all cases essentially their task of social education, whether as applying more particularly to the child himself or to his parents.

235.   Against that background, it seems to us that the juvenile panels must have available to them the services, first, of all the statutory and voluntary agencies whose work is such as to bring them into frequent contact with the family, and who may thus be looked upon as primary sources of identification. The police are obviously one such source; among others, perhaps the most obvious are the schools, general medical practitioners and the health visitor and district nursing services. The schools have, of course, close daily access to all children of school age. General medical practitioners, health visitors and district nurses (in some areas the two functions are combined) visit the great majority of homes where there are children under school age, and in many areas the health visitors may maintain a continuing link with the children in that they also form part of the school medical service. In what is in each case probably a numerically less extensive field, ministers and priests, children's officers, probation officers, local authority health and welfare officers, and school welfare and attendance officers in the course of their daily duties are also likely to identify children in need or difficulty. Under our proposals we contemplate that the social education department which we are recommending would be recognised as the focal point for co-ordination of information about all cases of children in need.

236.   Co-ordination of information leads to assessment or diagnosis. To be effective, the application of a process of social education of the kind we have described requires co-ordination of the various methods of treatment to be applied. We do not suggest that these can be carried out entirely within the social education department. We have already considered the part which the police may play in the process. Other services may not infrequently be concerned with the child's family or have a valuable contribution to the solution of the difficulties. At case-conferences attended by the various services concerned (voluntary and statutory) all the information available about the family, reported through the various identification agencies, would be considered. In the light of full assessment, carried out on a team basis, the most appropriate methods would be applied and the case assigned to the particular social worker or workers (within the total range of services) whose skills appeared to be best fitted to handle it. It follows that the director of social education would either have under his direct control or have a recognised right of access to, and claim upon, the specialist services (medical, psychiatric and psychological) in all cases in which such assistance appears appropriate.

237.   On completion of assessment, the resultant action may take any one of a variety of forms. As part of the general preventive function of the new service, the resultant measures would over a wide field be taken by simple administrative action, and measures of help and guidance would be entrusted to whichever was considered to be the most appropriate statutory or voluntary agency in the particular circumstances of the case. In cases in which for whatever reason it was considered necessary that there should be a formal referral to the juvenile panel, the panel's likely action on being satisfied that there was a need for their assuming jurisdiction would be to order either measures of supervision within the community or residential measures. The child's supervision within the community would in fact involve the application of family case-work and would, we envisage, be most commonly entrusted to the qualified social workers who would form a substantial element of the social education department operating directly under the director of social education. Similarly, where a child was removed from home by order of the panel for residential training (whether in the form of placing in the care of the local authority or for special residential school training of whatever kind) he would automatically be placed under the oversight and control of the social education department, subject to the additional requirement as to residential training. By that means remedial measures would, we think, necessarily be set in hand in the home simultaneously with the period of residential training, and supervision would be continued by the social education department for such period as might be considered necessary on the child's return home.

THE PRACTICAL SOLUTION

238.   In order to give effect to these principles, we consider that a measure of reorganisation of local social services is necessary. A major group of the services concerned, whether with identification, assessment or training, are at present within the education authority field, namely, the schools (including the school medical service and school welfare and attendance officers), the educational child guidance service, and residential schools (whether at present classed as schools for the maladjusted or the handicapped, as well as approved schools).

239.   Other residential homes and hostels are the responsibility of local authority children's committees, who are also responsible for the provision of remand homes which at present are intended to serve the function of assessment centres for children requiring in their own interests to be kept in custody pending appearance before the juvenile courts. Under our proposals assessment centres will essentially be places of safety. They will accommodate children whose needs appear to be of a degree of complexity requiring sustained assessment involving a variety of specialist services, and of a kind necessitating their temporary removal from home for this purpose—whether or not referral to the juvenile panel is in issue. As such, it is appropriate that the centres should under our proposals be under the direct control of the director of social education.

240.   So also, where on referral to the juvenile panel the child's supervision within the community is decided upon, it seems to us essential that there should be a single staff of field workers, working under the director of social education, to whom this task will normally be entrusted, and who will have the responsibility of assessing the effectiveness of the measures adopted in each

case. At present, supervision in such circumstances is most likely to be entrusted to a probation officer in the case of juvenile offenders, and in the case of others either to a probation officer or a children's officer. In this context both officers are undertaking what is essentially the same task as part of the process of social education implied in all family case-work, and the present arbitrary distinction which the selection of an officer of one or other of the two services seems to imply appears to us to have no basis in reality. Probation as a distinctive method of treatment of offenders has, however, from the outset been inevitably linked with the criminal courts. As one of the methods to be applied by the criminal courts it will, of course, continue. On that basis, under our proposals, the probation service as such will in future be related solely to the courts, and will occupy no similar special relationship with the juvenile panels, which would naturally look to the new social education department as the vehicle for exercising continued oversight and supervision of children under their jurisdiction.

THE SOCIAL EDUCATION DEPARTMENT

241. In the light of these considerations, we have reached the conclusion that the most effective practical organisation consistent with our general proposals lies in the reorganisation and merging of a number of local authority services to form a new "social education department", on the following lines:

(1) The present powers and duties of local authorities under the Children Acts, 1948 and 1958, and the Children and Young Persons Act, 1963, should be transferred to education authorities;

(2) Under the Director of Education, a new department should be set up, headed by a Depute Director (with the title of "Director of Social Education") who would head the new specialist department catering for the needs of all children requiring measures of special education and training. Within this larger organisation would be merged the existing child-care service as well as a substantial number of those at present serving in the probation service. With the removal of children from the jurisdiction of the criminal courts, the work of the latter service would be appreciably diminished, though in the longer-term the use of adult probation by the criminal courts may be expected to expand considerably beyond its present level;

(3) The education authority's existing responsibility for the educational child guidance service, the school medical services, for school welfare and attendance officers, as well as for the provision of special schools for the maladjusted and the handicapped, would be discharged through the new department;

(4) In consequence of the transfer of the child care functions of local authorities, responsibility for the provision of assessment centres and children's homes would be vested in education authorities, and would equally be operated under the direction of the new department, which by virtue of existing education authority functions would also be responsible for all existing and future special residential schools provided by the education authority;

(5) The approved school after-care service would be abolished and its functions merged within the social education department.

242. By that means the director of social education would have close to him or under his direct control—

(*a*)   a very large range of the services whose functions are such as to afford opportunities for the identification of children in need;

(*b*)   full facilities for assessment;

(*c*)   the necessary field organisation to undertake measures involving supervision (formal or otherwise) of children within the community; and,

(*d*)   the range of children's homes and residential schools provided by public authorities, as well as having access to similar homes and schools run by voluntary effort.

243.   These proposals, we recognise, involve a substantial measure of reorganisation, and go beyond the measures for co-ordination of services concerned with preventive measures recently enacted in the Children and Young Persons Act, 1963. Our recommendations basically imply an acceptance of the same underlying principles governing the machinery for identification, assessment and treatment as, we believe, led to these changes.

244.   We recognise that it might be thought that if there is in fact a need for further reorganisation it could appropriately be based, as are the 1963 Act changes, upon the children's committee of the local authority rather than by the creation of the new "social education" department under the education authority. Our proposals, however, imply a major extension of those working principles over a very much wider field, to include all children whose educational requirements are not met by the normal educational processes of the home and school (whether or not these needs are such as to postulate the assumption of jurisdiction by the juvenile panels). We have great difficulty in seeing how the very much larger organisation involved under our proposals could be founded upon the local authority children's committee, however that committee might be reorganised or its staff expanded. Such a proposal would in any event seem to imply the transfer to local authorities of a number of existing education authority functions (both relating to the child guidance service and residential schools), a course which would, we think, be unlikely to meet with any general measure of acceptance, and which for the reasons discussed in paragraphs 167–178, we ourselves would be quite unable to accept.

245.   A converse argument which might be advanced is that by placing responsibility for the new service in the hands of the education authority, there is a risk that the objects hoped for might not be achieved, in that the additional burden would add appreciably to those already existing in the general field of formal education and would thus end up by receiving inadequate attention. We do not consider that this view is well-founded. It may, we think, stem from an unduly narrow conception of what has always been and is increasingly being recognised as the true function of the public educational system. It may be that in the past the emphasis within the Scottish educational curriculum, with its fairly strongly academic bias, lent encouragement to the view that education could be treated as a formal process of learning, in that sense divorced from the wider aim of training for social living. In so far as such attitudes exist, they are, we consider, rapidly disappearing. In the immediate post-war years the attention of education authorities has necessarily been directed to the provision of improved facilities for general education as well as the additional provision required as a result of the raising of the school leaving age in 1947, the movement of population to new housing areas, and the continuing high birth

rate. On this account, it may be that their existing responsibilities for the ascertainment of the minority of children in special need (whether through maladjustment or handicap) were not pressed forward with the same vigour as might have been expected in other and more favourable circumstances. Equally, we think, the sub-division of responsibility implied by the creation of children's committees of local authorities may have acted as a disincentive to them to do so. In any event, the existence of the two Working Parties (to which we have already referred) on ascertainment of maladjustment and mental handicap is, we think, evidence of increased awareness and concern in educational circles for the special needs of these groups of children. Increasing emphasis on social education generally in more recent years is evident in education authorities' efforts to expand informal education, and in the rapid developments which have been taking place in junior secondary schools. Moreover, we do not think that the importance of organisational matters should be under-emphasized. Under our proposals, the "social education department" will in itself be a fairly large specialist department, headed under the Director of Education by a specialist Depute (holding what would be a mandatory statutory appointment in each area and carrying the salary and status appropriate to the rank of depute director of education). This appointment would in each case, we contemplate, be subject to the approval of the Secretary of State. A high career post of this kind would attract, both to the post and to service in the department, officers of high calibre, qualifications and experience.

A "Family" Service

246. In discussions before us, reference was made by some of the witnesses to the possibility in the long term of an even wider measure of reorganisation of services so as to provide a comprehensive "family service", catering for the needs of adults of all ages, as well as those of children in the family. Such a concept may have validity if it implies the need for better co-ordination of existing services, and we would expect that our own proposals, if adopted, would go a considerable way to improve the channels of communication necessary for concerted action relating to those, young or old, within a particular family unit, and irrespective of the initial source of referral. There is no doubt a need for further development of the existing services offering advice and guidance to adults in personal and other difficulties. Our own proposals, however, are necessarily directed primarily to the special needs of a minority of the child population who require special measures of education and training. These measures will almost always involve working closely with the parents; helping them to resolve their problems and sometimes those of other adult members of the family unit; and assisting them and strengthening their natural instinct to further the well-being of their children. We believe that society now and in the future will in fact be prepared to go to considerable lengths and considerable cost to further such a process of education for social living, holding as it does the possibility of sustained measures of care and discipline backed in many cases by the explicit authority of the juvenile panels. Such an approach is, we believe, a proper and appropriate one as catering for the needs of children, and in so far as the idea of a "family service" is a practical and achievable aim we consider that its centre and core will continue to be found in a "social education" service of the kind which we have recommended.

247. We recognise that our recommendations raise difficult questions as to the future of the probation service in particular, in that their immediate result will be likely to reduce its numbers, in so far as it will in future be a court-centred service concerned almost exclusively with adult offenders. We have reached our conclusions only after the most careful consideration, and we view with considerable regret the division which will necessarily result in an increasingly highly-trained organisation which has been painstakingly built up over the years. Under our proposals, we are, of course, looking to many serving officers of the probation service to fulfil an essential part by transfer to the new social education department. Transfer to the new service would, we contemplate, not be obligatory, and there would clearly require to be provision for compensation to particular officers in particular areas who did not elect to transfer, and who were as a result displaced from their present employment by reason of the new arrangements. (Arrangements to the same effect would be necessary in relation to serving officers of the approved schools after-care service.) We see no reason to consider that in the long term our proposals will be detrimental to the idea of probation as a method of treatment available for adult offenders, the use of which has been growing and may be expected to expand still further. The final resolution of questions about the future of the adult probation service goes well beyond our remit.

RECRUITMENT AND TRAINING

248. If these arrangements are to have maximum effect, we consider it essential that action should be taken at the earliest possible stage to establish recognised training standards within the various branches of the new department (both for field staff at a variety of levels and staff of residential homes and schools). Throughout the social services generally, there has in recent years been increasing recognition of the need to raise standards of training and to take full advantage of the body of theory and practical knowledge which has now become available in the field of social and personal relationships. The extent to which the social workers in the various existing services have undergone courses of training of this kind varies widely, as does the quality of the individual workers within each. In all fields the need for more systematic training has, however, been accepted; while the precise form of training machinery varies, a broad pattern has already emerged which can, we consider, appropriately be applied to service in the social education department which we have recommended.

249. In our view this should take the form of a statutory central training council or board, on which the education authorities, the central departments and the universities, as well as the social education department itself, would be represented. The council should by statute be entrusted with the task of laying down standards of recruitment and training for the various types of post within the department; of organising training courses; and of granting certificates of approval. One of its immediate tasks would be the provision of probationary courses for new recruits—satisfactory completion of which would be a prerequisite to the granting of the council's certificate of recognition. In our view it is essential that from the outset—at least in that substantial element of the department which will be employed in case-work—all new recruitment should proceed through such channels, and accordingly we recommend that statutory provision should be made whereby, from a date to be specified by the

Secretary of State, no person should be appointed to the social education department unless in possession of an appropriate training council certificate for the post to which he is to be appointed. We appreciate that, given the wide range of posts involved, it would probably be necessary to make provision enabling different dates to be specified for different sectors within the social education department. A further immediate as well as continuing task of the training council would be to provide refresher courses for serving officers. The general aim of all these arrangements is, of course, to raise training standards throughout the social education department to a recognised and accepted level within the shortest possible period; and, through the certificate-granting powers of the central training council, increasingly to accord to the new service the sense of professional status to which its skilled functions and exacting responsibilities entitle it.

CONCLUDING OBSERVATIONS

250.   We conclude our report by reverting to the issue posed at the end of Chapter III. Society is, we believe, seriously concerned to secure a more effective and discriminating machinery for intervention for the avoidance and reduction of juvenile delinquency. If so, it must in our view be prepared not only to recognise that the practical issue, as those to whom the task of adjudication is at present entrusted can readily confirm from daily experience, is indeed in every case the application of special measures of education and training appropriate to the needs of the individual child; but equally to recognise the consequences of that fact. These, as we have indicated, lie not only in the provision of effective machinery for early detection of situations which unchecked may lead to delinquency, and the application of remedial and educative processes at that stage. They also imply—where actual delinquency has occurred—an extension of that same machinery providing a similar flexibility and, at all stages, a continuity of oversight. Further, since the incidence of delinquency, the forms and patterns it takes, and in many cases the combination of factors apparently underlying it, vary widely from one area to another, these problems must in our view be tackled at local level and be clearly seen to be a local community responsibility. These aims cannot in our view effectively be met other than through, in each area, a locally-based agency publicly charged with specific responsibility for the prevention and reduction of juvenile delinquency. The social education department throughout the range of its activities, including the exercise of its continuing responsibility for children under the juvenile panels' jurisdiction, would in fact be such an agency.

251.   From the earliest age of understanding, every child finds himself part of a given family and a given environment—factors which are beyond his or society's power to control. During childhood the child is subject to the influences of home and school. Where these have for whatever reason fallen short or failed, the precise means by which the special needs of this minority of children are brought to light are equally largely fortuitous. The individual need may at that stage differ in degree, but scarcely in essential character, and such children may be said at present to be, more than most, in a real and special sense "hostages to fortune". The time has come, we believe, when society may reasonably be expected so to organise its affairs as to reduce the arbitrary effects of what is still too often a haphazard detection process; and consequently to

extend to this minority of children, within a sustained and continuing discipline of social education, the measures which their needs dictate, and of which they have hitherto been too often deprived.

Summary of Conclusions and Principal Recommendations

PART I

THE BASIC PROBLEM: ITS SCOPE AND THE PRACTICAL ISSUES ARISING

252. (1) In terms of the treatment measures to be applied, the children appearing before the courts, whatever the precise circumstances in which they do so, show a basic similarity of underlying situation. The distinguishing factor is their common need for special measures of education and training, the normal upbringing processes for whatever reason having failed or fallen short (paragraphs 6–15);

(2) The present treatment measures for these children are in the main based on an educative principle, which recognises the practical need for education and training, the underlying aim being to strengthen and further those natural influences for good which will assist the child's development into a mature and useful member of society;

(3) The most powerful and direct of these influences lies in the home, and such measures in practically every case thus involve, or ought to involve, working closely with the parents (paragraph 17);

(4) The importance of parental influence is universally recognised. This recognition sometimes leads to proposals for the application of direct sanctions, whether in the form of direct supervision, restitution or fines, on parents for their children's misdemeanours. Direct supervision on the parents implies a degree of direct personal responsibility as between parent and child which could seldom be established. Any proposal to make parents vicariously liable for their children's actions seeks to apply what are virtually criminal sanctions in situations falling far short of any recognised standard of neglect. Such proposals seem, moreover, to be incompatible with any idea of educational process. We are unable to accept the view that in matters so closely affecting their children, the co-operation and support of parents as adult persons can be enlisted by compulsory sanctions; a process of social education on the other hand implies working on a basis of persuasion which seeks to strengthen, support and further those natural familial instincts which are in whatever degree present in all parents (paragraphs 18–34);

(5) The evidence before us suggested that at a number of points the existing arrangements, while purporting to be based on an educative principle, are incompatible with such an approach. Instead of enlisting parental co-operation, they frequently tend to militate against it (paragraphs 35–38);

(6) If treatment of juvenile delinquents were to be accepted as properly being an educational process, then to be fully effective this would seem to require the formation in each area of a locally-based treatment authority, recognised as having specific responsibility for the prevention and reduction of juvenile delinquency; having either under its direct control, or having a recognised right of access to, all those local social services (public and

voluntary) primarily concerned with children's problems; having a direct and continuing responsibility for the children within its jurisdiction; and affording the fullest scope for enlisting the parents' co-operation and support for the measures applied at all stages;

(7)   Against that background we have had to examine how far the present arrangements fulfil these criteria, how far such shortcomings as may exist are attributable to mere defects of machinery or how far they are fundamental to the whole basis of the system of juvenile courts, and, in the light of such an examination, what appear to be the practical alternatives confronting society at the present time (paragraph 39).

THE UNDERLYING PRINCIPLES

The Juvenile Courts: Existing Arrangements

(8)   The constitution of the various types of juvenile courts in Scotland, and the arrangements which in various areas determine the choice of local court to which various classes of children are directed, appear to have been developed in response to particular local situations rather than on any consciously aimed principle. The common factor is that all are courts of summary jurisdiction, thus forming part of the machinery for the administration of criminal justice (paragraphs 40–50);

(9)   Criminal procedure is in essence concerned with the establishment of guilt or innocence and the punishment of the guilty, and thus assumes a high degree of personal responsibility in the individual. On the one hand, it is directed to the past act, and the punishment appropriate thereto; sentencing on the other hand also looks to the future. In so far as it is concerned with the future prevention of crime, sentencing thus introduces considerations which may in practice conflict with those already mentioned. In practice the present arrangements represent a compromise, and in relation to any individual offender the courts have to seek a balance on an empirical basis between the conflicting claims of the two principles. In so far as such a balance has to be maintained, it may in individual cases militate against early preventive measures, and against individualisation and subsequent alteration of treatment measures once applied (paragraphs 51–54);

(10)   The application of criminal procedure in the juvenile courts is, however, subject to further important qualifications, which have the effect of altering significantly the balance between the two principles already referred to, and which thus bring them, in the juvenile courts, even more sharply into conflict. The common law has always recognised, in relation to sentencing, that the element of youth may be a mitigating factor. More recent statute law has placed increasing emphasis on the need in every case to have regard to the child's future welfare and to secure those measures of education and training which are in his best interests. It requires the provision in all but the most trivial cases of social background information bearing on the child's home and family circumstances. These factors are clearly the practical expression of what is essentially a preventive or educational principle. The result, however, in many cases is that, whereas proceedings against children appear to start initially from some relatively minor act or default, when it comes to an assessment of the measures required, the juvenile court is expected to take into account circumstances right outside the complaint itself. As a result the treatment

measures may often appear to the parent and child as altogether out of proportion to the nature of the offence; even more important, the present arrangements may sometimes inhibit the application of measures which, on an educational principle, are clearly needed, but which cannot readily be justified on the basis of the offence viewed in isolation as a mere infraction of the criminal code (paragraphs 55–57);

The non-criminal jurisdiction of the juvenile courts

(11) This conflict is further highlighted by the fact that the juvenile courts, in addition to their criminal jurisdiction, exercise a non-criminal jurisdiction in respect of children in need of "care or protection". Proceedings of the latter kind operate on what is overtly a protective and educational principle. They may be instituted consequent on the parents' conviction of criminal neglect, or, short of that, on facts and circumstances amounting to situations of serious moral danger (actual or potential) to the child. Such situations are commonly recognised as being likely to contain all the elements of incipient delinquency. The underlying situation with which the courts are faced in such circumstances may often be almost indistinguishable from that in which they are called upon to deal with juvenile offenders; as a practical matter, the real issue is thus in every case the needs of the individual child, which can be assessed, and the appropriate treatment applied, only on an objective examination of the whole surrounding facts and circumstances. Yet it is inherent in criminal procedure, as applied to juvenile offenders, that it is in any given case in risk of militating unnecessarily against that process (paragraphs 58 and 59);

How the present arrangements have developed

(12) The personal and moral responsibility of children may vary widely, and a child's capacity to distinguish right and wrong, though developed at an early age, may not be accompanied by a corresponding degree of emotional maturity which would enable him to act on that knowledge. This has from the earliest times been reflected in the civil law relating to the rights and responsibilities of minors. While it has equally been accepted that the treatment of juvenile delinquency raises different considerations from those arising in the treatment of adult offenders, the criminal law assumes the responsibility of children other than those of tender years. This is expressed in the form of a legal presumption that no child under the age of 8 years is capable of criminal intent and thus cannot be made the subject of criminal proceedings. Such an age-limit is, however, clearly an arbitrary one and bears no relation to observable fact. The fact that it has been felt necessary to make such a distinction can be seen on closer examination not to reflect any absolute principle, but rather society's concern in earlier times to exclude children from the more extreme forms of punishment which conviction under criminal procedure formerly attracted, and whose application to children became increasingly repugnant to the public conscience. Subsequent legislation has had the effect of modifying substantially the rigours of the law so far as methods of treatment of juveniles are concerned, and has introduced a series of broad distinctions at later ages—the effect of which is to debar the application to children below those ages of various penalties and forms of custodial treatment. The major question, however, is not whether children under the age of 8 years are capable of acts of juvenile delinquency, and whether they should be made subject to a form of procedure plainly recognising that fact. The question is whether (*a*) the application of

criminal procedure to juvenile delinquents above that age has such compelling practical advantages as to outweigh the inherent disadvantages already discussed; or whether (*b*) in the interests of effective preventive measures, juvenile delinquents could be better dealt with under an entirely different form of procedure (paragraphs 60–67);

Suggestions for an alternative procedure

(13)   One solution suggested to us was that all children, whether classed at present as delinquents or as being in need of "care or protection", should be brought before the juvenile courts under non-criminal procedure, the basis of the petition being in all cases the child's need for protective and educational measures as shown by the whole surrounding circumstances, whether or not involving the commission of acts which, if done by an adult, would amount to crimes or offences. We are unable to recommend such a course, which would to some extent represent little more than a change of nomenclature. More important, however, where the basis of action rests on the commission of an offence, it is in our view of the utmost importance that any dispute about the facts alleged should continue to be determined on the presently accepted standards of evidence, and not on any lesser standard as would be the case if these matters were governed by what would be essentially a civil procedure (paragraphs 68–71);

A new alternative

(14)   The shortcomings inherent in the juvenile court system can, it seems to us, be traced essentially to the fact that they are required to combine the characteristics of a court of criminal law with those of a specialised agency for the treatment of children in need, whether in law juvenile offenders or children in need of "care or protection". It seems to us essential to separate clearly the two issues of (*a*) the resolution of any disputed issues of fact relating to the act or acts alleged, a task for which criminal procedure is well-fitted, and (*b*) consideration of the measures to be applied where the basic facts are established. Given the very limited extent to which the basic facts are in actual practice in any way in dispute, we see no insuperable difficulty in devising a machinery whereby all juvenile cases would be referred to a new and specialised treatment agency or panel, concerned solely with such measures on the basis of agreed referrals. The limited number of cases in which there was a dispute about the basic allegation would then at the outset be referred to a court of law which, if it upheld the allegation, would then remit to the panel for consideration of treatment measures as in any other agreed case (paragraphs 72-74);

(15)   The salient features of a juvenile panel of this kind would be that—

(*a*) it would be neither a court of law nor a local authority committee;

(*b*) it would be essentially a lay body, comprising persons who either by knowledge or experience were considered to be specially qualified to consider children's problems, a criterion on which none of the present systems of selection can be said from the outset to be based;

(*c*)   as the competent public agency vested with powers of compulsory action in this field, it should be seen to be an entirely independent agency, and the machinery of appointment should reflect that fact;

(*d*)   under such arrangements there would be no question of taking juvenile offenders outwith the ambit of the law. Such children would, a few exceptions apart, be dealt with not by criminal procedure but by a new form of public agency on whom this special jurisdiction would be conferred by law;

(e)   disputed issues of fact would be entirely outside the scope of the panels, being reserved for resolution by an appropriate court of law;

(f)   while the range of legal powers available to such an agency might not differ appreciably from those of the present juvenile courts, the manner in which they could competently be exercised would be markedly and fundamentally different. The criterion of action by such a panel in every case being the child's need for special measures of education and training, this implies a continuity of process which is altogether impracticable under existing arrangements, and which could be achieved only if (i) the panel were empowered to exercise a continuing jurisdiction over all children referred to them, subject only to a statutory upper age-limit, and (ii) within that period were accorded the widest discretion to alter, vary, or terminate the measures initially applied in the light of the child's progress and response;

(g)   the extension of continuing supervisory powers in this way would in certain cases clearly represent a substantially greater measure of intervention in matters affecting parent and child than is at present competent under the law. For this reason, wherever decisions by the panels were disputed by the parents, it would be essential that the latter should by law be afforded a right of appeal to an appropriate judicial authority (paragraphs 75 and 76);

(16)   Delinquency is predominantly an activity of the young. Ultimately the matter must be resolved on practical grounds. On purely practical grounds it would seem essential to provide for preventive and remedial measures at the earliest possible stage if more serious delinquencies are not to develop. Such measures cannot, it seems to us, operate with any reasonable expectation of success unless under a procedure which from the outset seeks to establish the individual child's needs in the light of the fullest information about his personal and family circumstances. The establishment of those needs is in itself a task calling for essentially personal qualities of insight and understanding, and for skills quite different from those involved in adjudicating legal issues. It seems to us inappropriate that a single agency should be expected to combine the two functions (paragraph 77);

(17)   The acceptance of an educational principle in this way implies a degree of continuity and flexibility of process which is impracticable under existing arrangements. It requires that juvenile panels (of the kind described) should be accorded, subject only to certain general limits laid down by law, the widest discretion initially in applying treatment measures, and in their subsequent variation, modification or termination in the light of the individual child's progress (paragraphs 78 and 79);

(18)   It must be a matter of judgment how far, in relation to juveniles and their parents, the application of an educational principle in this way would in fact and in practice represent an appreciable inroad into personal and family life, amounting to a degree of interference such as to be unacceptable in our society. If on such grounds it were to be felt that a fuller recognition of the educational principle could not be accepted, it is necessary to face the practical alternatives. A return to a purer form of the "crime–punishment" concept seems to us altogether unacceptable. If so, society must consider whether it is satisfied with

the *status quo* and is prepared to accept the social consequences. For out part we do not believe that a retention of the present system, resting as it does on an attempt to retain the two existing concepts in harness, is susceptible of modification in a way which would seem likely to have any marked impact on the problem. It is because we accept that society is indeed seriously concerned to secure effective measures for the prevention and reduction of juvenile delinquency, and because we consider that the method of approach which we are recommending has compelling practical advantages, that we have not hesitated to recommend major and radical changes (paragraphs 80 and 81).

Principal Recommendations

PART II

A NEW MACHINERY—THE JUVENILE PANELS

General

(19)(1) (*a*) Subject to the overriding discretion of the Crown (to be exercised exceptionally and for grave reasons of public policy) to prosecute in the Sheriff Court or the High Court of Justiciary, all juveniles under 16 should in principle be removed from the jurisdiction of the criminal courts;

(*b*) instead, juvenile panels should have power, on the grounds set out in paragraph 138, to assume jurisdiction over juveniles under 16 and to order special measures of education and training according to the needs of the juvenile concerned;

(*c*) disputed issues of fact relating to the grounds for assuming jurisdiction should be referred to the Sheriff; orders made by the panels should be subject to a right of appeal to the Sheriff;

(2) All existing juvenile courts should be abolished;

(3) The ordinary courts of summary jurisdiction should be the sole courts of summary jurisdiction for young offenders between the ages of 16 and 21;

(4) Provision for "care or protection" proceedings in relation to young people aged 16 and over should be abolished;

(5) Any rule of law or statutory provision establishing a minimum age of criminal responsibility should be repealed (paragraphs 82–139);

Constitution

(20) The juvenile panel or panels in each education area should be appointed by the Sheriff (paragraph 92);

Machinery for referrals

(21) Referral to the panel should in every case (irrespective of the basis or the initial source of the information) be at the instance of an independent official, to be known as the "reporter" to the panel (paragraphs 96–102);

(22) The right of the police, local authorities and other authorised persons to bring certain types of proceedings at their own instance should be abolished (paragraphs 98 and 99);

(23)   The preparation of social background reports, recommendations for treatment measures, and their subsequent application, should be the responsibility of a new statutory social education department, by virtue of its general function as the panel's executive agency (paragraphs 103 and 104);

(24)   The panels should be empowered to entertain only referrals in which the basic facts are agreed or admitted. The grounds of intervention where disputed should be subject to determination by the Sheriff Court. There should also be a right of appeal to the Sheriff (sitting as a judicial officer) against decisions of the panel; and to the Court of Session on questions of law arising from decisions by the Sheriff (paragraphs 110–114);

(25)   There should be a right of legal representation (and provision should where necessary be made for legal aid) in referrals or appeals to the Sheriff (paragraph 115);

(26)   Jurisdiction in all substantive treatment measures should be vested in the juvenile panel for the child's home area (paragraph 127);

Definition of the basis of the panel's jurisdiction

(27)   The jurisdiction of the panel should extend to any child of under 16 who is in need of special measures, education and training, in respect of whom, on a referral, one or more of the following circumstances are shown to apply, namely, his failing into bad associations or exposure to moral danger; his being the subject of criminal neglect or an unnatural offence (or being within the same household as such a child); his having violated the law as to crimes and offences; his being beyond control; his failure to attend school, whether by reason of truancy or parental refusal to comply with a requirement by the education authority as to attendance at a particular school; his parent or guardian having abandoned him or suffering from some permanent disability rendering him incapable of caring for the child, or who is of such habits or mode of life as to be unfit to have the care of the child (paragraphs 128–138);

Treatment measures

(28)   The treatment measures available to the juvenile panels should, as a matter of statutory powers, amount to the following:

(*a*)   decision to take no action;

(*b*)   admonition (with or without supervision);

(*c*)   finding of caution on the parent (normally with a supervision order on the child);

(*d*)   requirement that the child should attend at an attendance centre;

(*e*)   assumption of supervisory jurisdiction over the child—

(i)   where living at home; or

(ii)   where the situation so requires, including the additional requirement that he should be received into public care (and thus including, where necessary, residence in a children's home or residential school).

The foregoing relate to the panels' formal powers and are without prejudice to any measures that might be agreed informally with the parents, including the child's supervision on an informal basis (paragraphs 140–205);

Supervision within the community

(29) It is contemplated that supervision by the social education service would be the method of treatment most commonly applied by the juvenile panels. Within such a framework there will, however, be scope for supervision, formal or informal, by a variety of agencies. The police juvenile warnings system will continue to play a valuable part. Arrangements for informal supervision, under police juvenile liaison schemes, are equally to be commended. Since such schemes are essentially voluntary and informal, no rigid pattern is desirable, and other local experiments are to be encouraged (paragraphs 140–158);

Supervision involving special residential measures

(30) There is a serious need for further provision for special educational facilities (and especially residential schools) for children suffering from mental or physical handicap, or maladjustment. In particular, provision for the maladjusted child who also suffers from serious mental handicap is at present almost wholly lacking. There is also a shortage of hospital accommodation for children suffering from mental defect accompanied by serious emotional disturbance (paragraphs 172–177);

(31) The importance of early ascertainment of impaired intelligence and maladjustment, and appropriate special provision to meet such needs, is plain; and has an important part in the prevention and reduction of juvenile delinquency. Better provision in these directions would help to solve many of the problems within existing children's homes and residential schools (including approved schools). In so far as steps are planned or are already in train to remedy these shortages, we urge that they be pressed forward with all possible speed. A substantial need remains within the educational field (paragraph 178);

(32) The provision of special residential accommodation for all classes of children requiring special measures of education can in our view be assessed in proper balance and perspective only if handled by a single local authority, namely, the education authority, and the whole range of such provision should be available to the juvenile panels (paragraph 178);

(33) There is in particular a need for short-term residential school provision for pupils of junior secondary school-age who suffer from maladjustment; as well as separate residential provision for the training of younger boys (under 11) who, in the absence of more suitable provision, are at present accommodated in approved schools. New provision in these directions should in our view be made by education authorities (singly or in combination) rather than by additional approved school provision (paragraphs 187–189);

(34) Short-term detention (at present in remand homes) for children under 14 should be abolished. In so far as shorter-term residential training may be necessary for children aged 14–16 it can more appropriately be met within the special residential school provision which we have recommended (paragraphs 191–193);

Duration of orders

(35) The juvenile panels should have the widest discretion to vary subsequently the treatment measures initially applied. Subsequent variation, if

involving any greater measure of deprivation of parental rights, should be subject to a right of appeal to the Sheriff, and all orders should in any event be subject to a right of statutory appeal at annual intervals (paragraph 197);

Assessment

(36) We endorse the recommendation of the Ellis Committee for the development of assessment centres on a regional basis. Reporting to assessment centres and clinics for assessment purposes on an out-client basis should be encouraged. Assessment centres should be under the control of the social education department, which should be accorded a recognised claim on the time of specialist services (medical, psychological and psychiatric) (paragraphs 206–217);

Consequential matters

(37) Where children have acted in the company of adults charged with criminal offences, the former should, wherever practicable, be dealt with by the juvenile panels (paragraph 224);

(38) Where exceptionally children are the subject of proceedings in the criminal courts these courts should be empowered to remit to the appropriate juvenile panel for consideration of treatment measures (paragraph 224);

(39) Provision should be made for appointment in appropriate cases of full-time chairmen of juvenile panels; for lectures of training and instruction for panel members; and for payment of parents' expenses in cases of need in order to secure their attendance before the panels (paragraphs 225–230).

PART III

THE MATCHING FIELD ORGANISATION

(40) The existing statutory social services primarily concerned with children's problems should be reorganised so as to form a new comprehensive local department—to be known as "the social education department" (paragraphs 233–240);

(41) The most effective practical organisation consistent with our general proposals appears to us to entail the following:

(*a*) The present powers and duties of local authorities under the Children Acts, 1948 and 1958, and the Children and Young Persons Act, 1963, should be transferred to education authorities;

(*b*) Under the Director of Education, a new department should be set up, headed by a Depute Director (with the title of "Director of Social Education"). Within the larger organisation of this new specialist department, catering for the needs of all children requiring measures of special education and training, would be merged the existing child care service as well as a substantial number of those at present serving in the probation service. With the removal of children from the jurisdiction of the criminal courts, the probation service would cease to deal with children. Initially, the work of the latter service would thus be appreciably

107

diminished, though in the longer-term the use of adult probation by the criminal courts may be expected to expand considerably beyond its present level;

(c)   The education authority's existing responsibility for the educational child guidance service, the school medical service, and for school welfare and attendance officers would be discharged through the new department;

(d)   In consequence of the transfer of the child care functions of local authorities (already mentioned), responsibility for the provision of assessment centres and children's homes would be vested in education authorities, and would equally be operated under the direction of the new department, which by virtue of existing education authority functions would also be responsible for all existing and future special residential schools provided by the education authority;

(e)   The approved schools after-care service should be abolished, its function in future being discharged by the social education department as part of its general supervisory role in relation to all children under the juvenile panel's jurisdiction (paragraph 241);

(42)   Arrangements should be made for compensation for those social workers in the probation service and the approved schools after-care service displaced from employment as a result of the new arrangements and not re-employed in the social education service (paragraph 247);

(43)   A statutory central training council should be established with responsibility for recruitment and training in the various branches of the social education department. It should be accorded certificate-granting powers. Provision should be made enabling the Secretary of State to fix a date or dates after which no person will be eligible for various classes of appointments in the social education department unless in possession of the appropriate certificate of recognition issued by the training council (paragraphs 248 and 249);

Concluding observations

(44)   Society is, we believe, seriously concerned to secure a more effective and discriminating machinery for intervention for the avoidance and reduction of juvenile delinquency. If so, it must in our view be prepared not only to recognise that the practical issue is indeed in every case the application of special measures of education and training appropriate to the needs of the individual child, but equally to recognise the consequences of that fact. These lie not only in the provision of effective machinery for early detection of situations which unchecked may lead to delinquency, and the application of remedial and educative processes at that stage. They also imply, where actual delinquency has occurred, an extension of that same machinery providing a similar flexibility and, at all stages, a continuity of oversight. They further imply the possibility of sustained process by the application of more intensive training measures where necessary for considerable periods. Moreover, since the incidence of juvenile delinquency, the forms and patterns it takes, and in many cases the combination of factors apparently underlying it, vary widely from one area to another, these problems must in our view be tackled at local level and must be clearly seen to be a local community responsibility. These aims cannot in our view effectively be met other than through, in each area, a locally-based agency publicly charged with specific responsibility for the prevention and reduction of juvenile delinquency. The social

education department, throughout the range of its activities (including the exercise of its continuous responsibility for children under the juvenile panel's jurisdiction) would in fact be such an agency.

From the earliest age of understanding, every child finds himself part of a given family and a given environment—factors which are beyond his or society's power to control. During childhood the child is subject to the influences of home and school. Where these have fallen short or failed, the precise means by which the special needs of this minority of children are brought to light are equally largely fortuitous. The individual need may at that stage differ in degree, but scarcely in essential character, and such children may be said at present to be, more than most, in a real and special sense "hostages to fortune". The time has come, we believe, when society may reasonably be expected so to organise its affairs as to reduce the arbitrary effects of what is still too often a haphazard detection process; and consequently to extend to this minority of children, within a sustained and continuing discipline of social education, the measures which their needs dictate, and of which they have hitherto been too often deprived (paragraphs 250 and 251).

(Sgd.) C. J. D. SHAW (*Chairman*)

JOHN C. BALFOUR	HAMILTON LYONS
W. HEWITSON BROWN	ANDREW MELDRUM
L. P. CAMERON-HEAD	NORMAN MURCHISON
C. S. HAMPTON	MARY W. REILLY
RONALD IRELAND	F. H. STONE
MARGARET H. KIDD	ALLAN G. WALKER

A. T. F. OGILVIE, Secretary
R. J. EDIE, Assistant Secretary
10*th January*, 1964

109

APPENDIX 'A'

CRIMINAL STATISTICS, SCOTLAND

Juveniles (aged 8 to 16 inclusive) against whom charges were proved with or without a finding of guilt—1950–1962

| YEAR | BOYS | | GIRLS | | BOYS AND GIRLS | | | |
| | Total | Per 1,000 of population aged 8–16 (inclusive) | Total | Per 1,000 of population aged 8–16 (inclusive) | Total | Per 1,000 of population aged 8–16 (inclusive) | Previously found guilty Number | Percentage of column 6 |
(1)	(2)	(3)	(4)	(5)	(6)	(7)	(8)	(9)
1950	16,247	44.9	834	2.4	17,081	23.9	2,891	16.9
1951	16,350	47.3	986	2.8	17,336	24.8	2,730	15.7
1952	15,819	44.8	1,023	3.0	16,842	24.1	2,685	15.9
1953	15,430	43.5	1,083	3.1	16,513	23.6	2,523	15.3
1954	14,752	41.5	873	2.5	15,625	22.3	2,300	14.7
1955	14,629	38.7	908	2.5	15,537	21.4	2,401	15.4
1956	14,530	38.6	799	2.2	15,329	20.7	2,386	15.6
1957	15,213	39.8	914	2.5	16,127	21.5	2,437	15.1
1958	16,404	42.3	1,042	2.8	17,446	23.0	3,023	17.3
1959	17,542	44.9	983	2.6	18,525	24.2	3,098	15.9
1960	19,134	49.0	1,172	3.1	20,306	26.5	3,404	16.8
1961	20,413	52.8	1,333	3.6	21,746	28.7	4,033	18.5
1962	20,357	52.3	1,555	4.2	21,912	28.7	4,007	18.5

111

Parental Liability in Civil Law for the Wrongful Acts of Minors

1.   The essential principle of Scots law is that a parent is not liable in respect of damage caused by his child unless he himself has been at fault.

2.   It is necessary first to make a distinction between direct and vicarious liability. A defender may be liable for a delict either by doing the act himself (as by negligently driving his own motor car) or by contributing by his own fault to a wrong physically caused by someone else (as by allowing a child of 5 to take the wheel of his motor car). These are both cases of direct liability. On the other hand, a defender may be vicariously liable for the act of another although he himself has not been in fault at all. Thus the employer of a servant who commits a delict in the course of his employment is liable in damages, although he is not personally involved in the delict and has taken all proper care to choose a competent servant.

3.   Vicarious liability, defined in this way, is a comparatively modem development, and was adopted in Scots law only in the nineteenth century. There was no such doctrine in Roman law, although the peculiarities of the law of noxal liability have tended to obscure this fact. In Roman law the master of a slave who wrongfully caused damage could not be compelled to pay damages unless he himself had been at fault, either by directly authorising the wrong, or because he had been negligent in his choice of slave (*culpa in eligendo*). In either of these exceptional cases the master was liable, but he was liable directly and not vicariously. In all other cases, where the master had not been at fault, he could not be compelled to pay damages, but the injured party was entitled to seize the slave who had caused the damage and keep him as his own property (in early law, when civil and criminal liability were not well distinguished, the object of this was to enable him to wreak vengeance on him). In such a case the master had the right to buy off the slave by paying the amount of the damage. He was under no liability to do so; it was his privilege to do so if he thought that the amount due was worth paying in order to continue to have the services of his slave.

4.   Originally these rules applied to all persons who were in the *potestas* of the *paterfamilias*—i.e., not only to slaves but also to children. Thus in classical law a free man who was a *filiusfamilias* could be seized by a person to whom he had wrongfully caused damage in the same way as a slave, with an option to the father to buy him off if it was worth it. The only difference was that the free *filiusfamilias* had to be released once he had worked off the amount of the damage. In the later Roman law, when it was quite usual for a *filiusfamilias* to have money of his own which could be used to pay damages, the pursuer's right to seize the person of a free delinquent disappeared.

5.   The Roman law may be summarised by saying that in all cases the actual delinquent was liable to make reparation, either financially in the case of a free person *sui juris*, or by personal servitude in the case of a person without

property, whether he was a slave or, in the older law, a *filiusfamilias*. This second type of liability could be commuted in the option of the *paterfamilias*, but he was never under any vicarious liability.

6. The earlier Scots law seems to have taken over the Roman law rule that a defender could be made liable only if he had been himself in fault, either by causing the damage himself, or, if it had been caused physically by someone else, by some contributory fault in choosing or controlling the actual delinquent. There is nothing resembling noxal liability in the common law of Scotland, although there is an interesting example of statutory noxality in the Act of 1503 c. 12 (A.P.S. ii 242). This is in the following terms (spelling has been modernised as far as possible):

> ITEM anent stealers of rabbits or pikes out of stanks, breakers of dovecots or orchards or stealers of beehives and destroyers thereof and also anent them that slay deer or roes or roebucks of lords' proper woods that that be a point of dittay in time to come and that the unlaw[1] thereof be £10 together with amends to the party[2] according to the scathe, and if any children within age commit any of these things foresaid because they may not be punished for not lawful age[3] their fathers or masters shall pay for ilk ane of them ilk time committing any the trespass foresaid 13s. 4d. or else deliver the said child to the judge to be lashed, scourged and dung[4] according to his fault.

7. This, however, is merely an amusing curiosity. The common law on the liability of a master for his servant's wrong continued on Roman lines—i.e., he was liable if he had been in fault, and not otherwise. Lord Kames (*Principles of Equity* (3rd ed., 1778)) deals with the liability of a defender to make reparation for damage caused by "persons, animals and things under his power". No specific mention is made of children:

> "With respect to servants, it is the master's business to make a right choice, and to keep them under proper discipline; and therefore, if they do any mischief that might have been foreseen and prevented, he is liable."

Of the institutional writers only Bankton, whose *Institute* was published in 1751–53, mentions children specifically as wrongdoers for whom a parent may be liable. At first sight it may seem that he is laying down a rule of strict vicarious liability both for servants and for children (I, x. 47):

> "By the present custom, if damage is done by children in family, or servants, in the offices or business in which they are employed, their father or master is liable to repair it."

But it is clear from what follows (1) that there is liability for children only in so far as they can be regarded as servants (i.e., that the words "in the offices or business in which they are employed" refer to children as well as to servants, and (2) that Bankton is not really dealing with vicarious liability, but merely with liability for authorised acts:

> "But otherwise, the children or servants are only answerable themselves for damage done, without the parent's or master's authority; and, if with it, the parent or master only, and not the children or servants who were bound to obey."

---

1 *unlaw*: a fine.
2 *the party*: the party injured.
3 i.e. because they may not be punished by reason of the fact that they are not of lawful age.
4 *dung*: p.p. of *ding*. This fine word has a general connotation of "beat" or "harass" or "push around". See the Scottish National Dictionary s.v.

8.   There is, so far as we have been able to trace, no later authority until the two Outer House decisions in the twentieth century, with which we deal below. Accordingly, there can be little doubt that in Scots law a father is liable for his child **as such** only if there has been a culpable failure to prevent damage which the father ought to have foreseen. The mystery indeed is not why there is no vicarious liability for children, but how the law has succeeded in introducing vicarious liability for servants. A full discussion of this would be out of place here, but it seems to have crept in, early in the nineteenth century, as a measure of policy rather than as the result of any conscious principle. Indeed, even as late as 1877 it was regarded as a departure from principle, and to be justified only on the ground of convenience (sc. to the pursuer who would otherwise fail to recover damages). See the opinion of Lord Shand in *Woodhead* v. *Gartness Mineral Co.* ((1877) 4R. 469, 508).

9.   The two more recent decisions in the Outer House do not advance the matter at all. They were both concerned with an attempt to make a father liable for damage caused by a son over the age of puberty while driving the father's motor car. But in neither was any attempt made to suggest that the father could be vicariously liable for his son. The basis of the pursuer's case was that the father was liable as a principal for the authorised act of his agent, and in the earlier of the two cases, *McKay* v. *McLean* (1920 1 S.L.T. 34), Lord Anderson brushed aside any suggestion that the relationship by itself could have created liability:

> "It is plain, I think, that it is an immaterial circumstance that the driver of the car was the defender's son; the question would have been just the same had the driver been a stranger in blood to the defender."

Police Juvenile Liaison Schemes

THE LIVERPOOL SCHEME

(The notes which follow are, by permission, reproduced from the booklet, *The Police and Children*, published by the Chief Constable of Liverpool—Second Edition, 1962.)

---

1. Following the second world war and the alarming rise in all forms of crime including that committed by juveniles, we considered that much more could and should be done in a positive way to prevent children from becoming delinquents and in guiding those who had come to our notice through misbehaviour in such a way as to prevent them from getting into further trouble. In 1950 the problem was carefully surveyed and of the school population of some 125,000 it was found that the number of crimes known to the police as having been committed by juveniles was 2,248 which represented 1.8 per cent of all the children of school age in the city. It may not seem a very high percentage, but when compared with the percentage of crime which had been committed by the adult population, i.e., 0.5 per cent, the problem was distinctly disturbing.

2. One very significant feature which also emerged was the fact that a large number of criminal offences committed by juveniles were not being brought to the notice of the police. Many children caught shoplifting and committing other forms of pilfering were not reported to the police because, as the manager of one very large departmental store explained, "they could not provide sufficient staff to go through the procedure of attending Court in all such cases and the recovery of the stolen property at the time was the most satisfactory way of dealing with the matter". However, the ultimate result of this policy meant that many children thought they were getting away without punishment for their misbehaviour and continued stealing until, inevitably, they came into the hands of the police. Quite often by this stage their moral values had been tainted.

3. Our pilot experiment of juvenile liaison officers was brought into being whereby the co-operation was sought of the various shops, stores, warehouses, etc., in order that all juveniles caught pilfering were notified to the police without discrimination. With the co-operation of parents and the help and advice of teachers and the various social services, it was decided that as soon as the police were aware that a child had committed an offence for the first time, and it was not a serious one, and provided the offender admitted the facts and the owner of the property or persons offended against did not wish to prosecute, then the specially selected and trained officer would, with the full co-operation of parents, take the child under his aegis. Our specific object was to prevent a recurrence of this bad behaviour.

4. The success of this pilot venture led to the establishment in 1952 on a firm basis of the Juvenile Liaison Department and its incorporation as part of the Crime Prevention Branch of the Liverpool City Police. It is now staffed by two

sergeants, seventeen constables (including four policewomen) under the supervision of a Chief Inspector.

5. The selection of these officers is made from personnel who have applied to be considered for the work. They must be able, experienced, possess the qualities of understanding and leadership; and they must have had a considerable background and experience in youth work. A searching assessment is made of each candidate and those selected undergo a period of training under the guidance of an experienced juvenile liaison officer in the field. As vacancies occur the most suitable candidate is appointed. All the officers work in plain clothes and devote their full time to every aspect of juvenile crime. They are allowed a reasonably wide discretion in adopting any measure which might be expected to benefit the child.

6. The success of the scheme depends on the whole-hearted co-operation of all who are interested in the direction and welfare of children, and it is the duty of each juvenile liaison officer to:

(*a*) Establish and maintain a close liaison with head teachers, ministers of religion, youth club leaders, and any other persons in their respective divisions who are interested or concerned in the welfare of children or young persons.

(*b*) Collaborate with the probation service without usurping or overlapping any of its functions.

(*c*) Keep individual records of juveniles dealt with or who have come to the notice of the police in respect of offences committed by them.

(*d*) Maintain a regular contact with juveniles cautioned by the police, and their parents.

7. Regular monthly conferences are held by the Chief Constable at which all the officers must attend to discuss policy and the various human problems which inevitably arise and which must be resolved.

8. Juvenile liaison officers are empowered to deal with all children and young persons:

(1) Under the age of 17 years;

(2) Who have committed a minor offence of stealing or something similar (*N.B.*—crimes of breaking and entering premises are not considered minor offences);

(3) Who admit the offence;

(4) Who have not previously come to the notice of the police; and

(5) Whose parents agree to co-operate with the police by accepting any help and advice about the child's future.

9. The decision whether to prosecute a child or to administer a caution and refer him to the juvenile liaison officer is made by the Assistant Chief Constable (Crime), and generally it is the policy to caution rather than prosecute a juvenile who is known to be a first offender and who comes within the above category. Of course, account must be taken of the whole circumstances of each individual case, e.g., the degree of temptation, and any aggravating or ameliorating factors.

10. Juveniles dealt with under the scheme are divided broadly into two classes:

(*a*) children who have committed an offence; and

(*b*) potential delinquents.

11. The first category come to the juvenile liaison officer through the normal police channels of the Uniform Branch and Criminal Investigation Department, and are cautioned by the Divisional Chief Superintendent in whose division the offence was committed. Afterwards, the juvenile liaison officer has a talk to the parents, explains to them the facilities of the scheme and, provided they are willing, accepts the child into the scheme. If the parents refuse to co-operate, the juvenile liaison officer simply withdraws from the case. Happily, this rarely happens; the majority of the parents are only too willing to take advantage of his help.

12. The second class, the potential delinquents, are children who are not known to have committed any offence, but are brought to the notice of the juvenile liaison officers by their parents, teachers, or by other police officers, for consistently playing truant, becoming unruly and out of hand at home or school, staying out late at night, behaving in a disorderly manner, or frequenting undesirable places—in other words, juveniles whose behaviour is considered morally harmful and which, without correction, might develop into criminal tendencies.

13. Naturally, in its initial stages, the scheme encountered a certain amount of distrust, particularly from a certain strata of parents who found it difficult to believe that the work of these particular policemen and women was designed to help to keep their children out of trouble rather than to prosecute them. By good faith and patience this barrier has gradually been overcome, and the better under-standing and experience of the work and the growth of the numbers dealt with as potential delinquents illustrates the improved understanding which now exists.

14. In addition to these two categories, the juvenile liaison officers at the request of parents and teachers often give a timely but friendly word of warning or advice. In 619 instances this was done in 1960 and our actions in relation to these and potential offenders reflect the extent of crime prevention work which is being done amongst the young people of the city.

15. The juvenile liaison officer is there to assist the parents with their child, not to supervise. On receiving a case he makes every effort to learn the background of the boy or girl and discover the underlying reasons for the offence. Its seriousness is impressed on both the offender and on the parents, and arrangements are made with the father and mother for a period of care and guidance, which naturally varies according to the child and its home environment. The officer's object is to foster in the mind of the child ideas which will lead to responsible citizenship and, where necessary, bring home to the parents their individual responsibilities.

16. With the parents' consent, the head teacher of the child's school is informed of the facts of the case and the officer's proposed course of action. In this way additional and helpful information is obtained about the character and behaviour of the child at school. Should the cause of the trouble have originated from within the school, for example, from the formation and participation in a gang, the school master assists by helping to break up the association and keep a special supervision on the child's conduct during schooltime; if the child is a practising member of a religious denomination, his minister may be approached to see if he can give any further help; and if he is a member of a youth club, the leader may be able to assist. Where a child not a member of any organisation wishes to join one and the officer considers that he or she would benefit,

arrangements are made for the child to be introduced to a youth club. From time to time he visits the child's home, talks to the parents and the child, visits the school, observes the child at play, until it is clear that his help is no longer needed and only then does he close the case.

17. Juvenile liaison officers keep their records in the form of individual case papers which record reports of visits, etc., together with other useful details regarding the offence, character and home background of the offender. They limit their role of social workers to maintaining a liaison between parents, schools, clubs, ministers and voluntary services.

18. The majority of children committing offences initially are naughty little boys invariably from families whose parents have not taken the slightest interest in teaching them the difference between right and wrong. These simple cases detected in the early stages are the ones dealt with by the juvenile liaison officer, and it is he, with the help of the school teacher, minister and the club leader, who remedies this deficiency in parental responsibility. Often this is all that is necessary to effect a "cure".

19. If there is the slightest suspicion that a child requires more specialised treatment, the officer hands the case over to the appropriate authority who is much more competent to deal with it, such as the School Medical Officer, Child Guidance Clinic, or the Psychiatric Department of the Children's Hospital, etc.

20. On many occasions the liaison officers are called upon to address children in schools on "Citizenship" and at certain "critical" times of the year such as immediately prior to Guy Fawkes night and the regular school holidays, they tour the schools advising children about their behaviour. They are regularly invited to meetings of Parent–Teacher Associations, thus maintaining a sympathetic and balanced relationship.

21. Every juvenile liaison officer has been co-opted to a number of committees whose work concerns the youth of the city, including those of the Youth Welfare Association, inaugurated by the Youth Welfare Advisory Committee under the patronage of the Director of Education which comprises members of the different social organisations interested in young people.

22. Close personal contact is thus maintained with the leaders and members of all youth clubs in their divisions and their help has frequently been requested at annual camps and at courses held for unemployed youth. In areas where facilities for the physical development of children and young people have been found to be inadequate, our officers have done much to provide for these children acceptable and satisfying leisure-time activities.

23. There is a happy and helpful liaison and mutual regard between our officers and those of the Children's Department, Probation Service, National Society for the Prevention of Cruelty to Children, etc. If on making his initial enquiry at a home, the juvenile liaison officer discovered that one of these services is already actively interested, he immediately makes contact with the appropriate officer to explain our interest and then withdraws from the case. No juvenile liaison officer is authorised to maintain visits to homes at which other authorities are calling.

24. Liverpool is most fortunate in its many valuable voluntary social services, all of whom readily assist in this police service. Indeed, it must be

emphasised that the Juvenile Liaison Scheme could not have been such a success without the unselfish support and co-operation given to it by all the voluntary and statutory social services in the city, and especially the help and encouragement of the Director of Education.

25. The scheme has now been in operation in Liverpool for 10 years. A tremendous amount of work has been enthusiastically performed by the juvenile liaison officers, and there is no doubt that a great deal of good has been done. The success of social and preventive work cannot be measured entirely from statistics, and in any case, it was never envisaged that dramatic reductions in the figures for juvenile crime could be effected quickly. The successes achieved will seldom come to light and will be known only to those intimately concerned, but sufficient has been seen to prove that the employment of these officers is more than justified, and that but for their services many more children would have drifted into delinquency and ultimately to crime.

APPENDIX 'D'

Relationship between the Police and the Schools

1. A scheme was introduced by the Chief Constable of Nottingham in November, 1961, with the approval and co-operation of the Director of Education and the Education Committee, the aim being—

"to promote a better understanding between children and the police, by arranging visits to schools lasting for a week or more, and introducing to the children, officers from the various police departments and their equipment, at the same time stimulating and assisting them in an educational project with "The Police" as the focal point."

2. The Scheme is conducted and supervised by a Detective Sergeant who is the Crime Prevention Officer at Force Headquarters.

3. The Sergeant meets the head teacher and staff of the school and outlines the Scheme, which has become known as "Police Week". He conducts the teaching staff on a tour of Police Headquarters and of the courts, and explains the functions of the various departments. This prior knowledge helps teachers considerably in their individual approach to "Police Week" in relation to the particular age-group of their class.

4. One week prior to "Police Week", the Sergeant talks to the whole school after morning Service and tells them about the Scheme and what is expected of everyone taking part. From that moment the children begin to collect library books, and other material about the police, and the teaching staff arrange for all lessons to have a police flavour, for example, maths might include radio car mileage, cost of maintaining police horses and dogs, their height, weight, breed and uses etc., distance travelled by radio patrols, and so on. A little science on the origin of radio, and how it is used by the police; such things as marine life from the frogman; and models and pictures as part of art lessons. A display is arranged in the school hall consisting of police photographs covering every section, equipment such as old and new handcuffs, truncheons, helmets, lamps, old prison keys, police riot rattles, whistles, and education and law books used by police and cadets.

5. Monday morning comes and the Sergeant arrives at the school in uniform, just before 9 o'clock, and joins the children and staff at Morning Prayers. During the first day he has a class at a time in the school hall, near the display, and talks to them about a variety of subjects, at the same time impressing upon them that the policeman is always a friend of children, **but** there are times when he has to exercise his authority as an officer of the law. This is the theme throughout the week. He outlines the history of the police, their training and work, going on to speak of offences and nuisances which some children commit, such as trespassing in buildings, on railways, or building sites, damaging property and trees, bullying, cruelty to animals, dangers on the road, the correct use of the "999" system, youth clubs, lost and found property and the

dangers of taking rides with strangers in motor vehicles. They are reminded of the importance of self respect; respect for parents and teachers; prestige of their school, punctuality, helping old people and younger or handicapped children, in other words, the way to good citizenship.

6.   During the week the children write about the police and their work and are visited by other officers, including detective officers, policewomen and cadets, who come into the school and talk to them about their particular duties in the Force, including demonstrations by police dogs, horses, frogmen, radio cars, and motor cycles. The week comes to an end and the Sergeant takes leave of all the many friends (staff and children) he has made at the school.

7.   A few days later he sends police transport to bring a party of children to Police Headquarters where they are shown round. They are also taken to the police stables, police dog training school, and to a new sub-divisional police station.

8.   Afterwards, the interest of the children in the police is maintained by a uniformed officer who "adopts" the school and looks in every 6 weeks, offering his services to the headmaster in a variety of ways, e.g., refereeing or controlling sporting events, talking to children in class about seasonal topics such as dangers of rivers, boating, gravel pits, bonfires and fireworks, etc. This officer is known as the "Continuation Officer". He is a volunteer with a keen interest in and a flair for this class of work. There is no shortage of applicants. The most rewarding aspect of this scheme is the interest taken both by the teaching staff and the children; and the vast amount of written and pictorial work produced by the scholars, with many delightful drawings of police dogs, horses, cars, graphs and models etc.

9.   It is appreciated that the benefits from a scheme of this kind, designed to produce a close and friendly association with the police at an impressionable age will take some time to develop, but the ultimate outcome cannot fail to produce some good and lasting effect upon children during the process of growing-up, and be a guiding influence to them in later years, when faced with moments of decision, danger or temptation. At first, there was some doubt amongst teaching staff as to the need for the police to come into school for a whole week; and the reactions of parents were also considered. All these things were discussed and settled at the original planning stage. It can now be said that the scheme has been wholeheartedly received by everyone and so far there has been no adverse criticism of any kind. On the contrary, the Chief Constable has received many letters of praise from head teachers and from parents, and there is not the slightest doubt that the scheme has been a great success in Nottingham, and becomes even more successful as time goes on.

List of organisations and individuals who submitted statements of evidence

Notes— (1) Oral as well as written evidence was given by those marked*.
(2) Those marked † gave oral evidence in other capacities.

(a) Organisations

Aberdeen City and County Society for the Prevention of Cruelty to Children.
*Approved Schools Association (Scotland).
*Association of Child Care Officers (Scottish Region).
*Association of County Councils in Scotland.
*Association of Directors of Education in Scotland.
*Association of Sheriffs Principal.
*British Medical Association (Scottish Council).
*British Psychological Society.
*British Transport Commission.
*Chief Constables' (Scotland) Association.
*Chief Constables of Greenock, Coatbridge. Stirlingshire and Clackmannan.
*Church of Scotland Committee on Social Service.
*Committee of Management, Edinburgh Home for Mothers and Infants.
Counties of Cities Association.
*Department of Social Study, Edinburgh University.
*Edinburgh Voluntary Youth Welfare Association.
*Educational Institute for Scotland.
*Episcopal Church in Scotland (Joint Committee of the Board of Education
      and the Social Services Board).
*Howard League for Penal Reform (Scottish Branch).
Institute of Housing (Scottish Branch).
*Law Society of Scotland.
*National Association of Probation Officers (Scottish Branch).
*Procurators Fiscal Society.
Professional Case-workers Working Party.
*Royal Medico-Psychological Association (Scottish Division).
*Royal Scottish Society for the Prevention of Cruelty to Children.
Salvation Army in Scotland.
*Scottish Approved Schools Staff Association.
*Scottish Children's Officers' Association.
*Scottish Committee of the Catholic Union of Great Britain.
*Scottish Education Department.
*Scottish Health Visitors' Association.
Scottish Home and Health Department.
*Sheriffs-Substitute Association.
Society of Civil Servants (Sheriff Clerks' Branch).
*Society of Medical Officers of Health (Scottish Branch).
*Society of Town Clerks in Scotland.

(b) Individuals

The Hon. Lord Cameron, D.S.C., LL.D.
*Mr. Arthur S. Fraser, Headmaster, Fernieside School, Edinburgh.
 Mr. Robert Goodburn, Clerk of the Peace for Peeblesshire.
*Mr. J. D. Heatly, City Prosecutor, Edinburgh.
 Mr. J. C. T. MacRobert, Clerk of the Peace for Renfrewshire.
 Mr. Andrew Lawson, J.P., Glasgow.
 Town Clerk and the Children's Officer, Motherwell and Wishaw.
 Town Clerk†, the Children's Officer and the Probation Officer, Kirkcaldy.

†Dr. K. R. H. Wardrop, M.A. CH.B., D.P.M.
†Dr. J. P. McWhinnie, M.B., CH.B., D.C.H., D.P.M.   A professional group of
 Mr. R. C. Vallance, M.A., ED.B.   consultants and psychiatric
 Miss Muriel Humphries, B.A.   social workers working in
†Mr. David Colvin   Scottish approved schools
 Miss Muriel Linda Hunt, B.A.   and borstals.

 Mrs. Elizabeth Wilson, Wishaw.

INDEX

Printed in Great Britain for HMSO Scotland by
CC No 20249 IOC 6/95